MANDY MARROW

Copyright Statement

Legal Disclaimer

MOCKTAILS MASTERY

TABLE OF CONTENT

Discover your mocktail magic!

CITRUS AND SPARKLING CREATIONS 13

HERBAL AND TEA INFUSIONS 42

SODAS AND FIZZY CONCOCTIONS 71

TROPICAL PARADISES 22

CREAMY AND DESSERT MOCKTAILS 52

SEASONAL SPECIALS 82

BERRIES AND FRUIT MIXES 32

CLASSIC MOCKTAILS MADE SIMPLE 62

QUICK AND EASY 5-INGREDIENT MOCKTAILS 92

MOCKTAILS

Ever sipped a drink so invigorating, so delicious, that you can almost hear the fizz of effervescence or the soft clink of the ice, even long after the glass is empty? Yet, imagine that very drink being devoid of any alcoholic content but packed with flavor, freshness, and flair. Welcome to the vibrant world of mocktails!

We've all been there. Social occasions where you want the joy of a cocktail without the alcohol. Maybe it's a lunch meeting, a health choice, or you're the designated driver. It could be a festive occasion where children and non-drinkers want to feel included in the celebration. Whatever your reason, there's a growing need for beverages that are as fun and sophisticated as their alcoholic counterparts.

Embracing mocktails doesn't mean giving up your favorite beverages or flavors. It's about discovery—a new realm of taste, creativity, and presentation. Once you venture into the world of mocktails, you'll realize they're more than just a blend of juices. They are an experience. A dance of flavors, if you will, that promises a refreshing escape with every sip.

Now, you might wonder, why trust me? Having spent years behind the bar, mixing, shaking, and presenting thousands of beverages, I've seen firsthand the evolving preference of customers. I've watched the rise of mocktails from mere 'add-ons' in the menu to stars of the show. With my expertise and passion for crafting beverages, I'm here to guide you through this flavorful journey, shedding light on techniques, ingredients, and the art of presentation.

In the upcoming chapters, you'll uncover not just recipes, but stories, inspirations, and the 'why' behind each drink. So, as we set the stage and you adjust your apron, prepping to dive deep into this tantalizing world, let's ponder on a fundamental question in our next chapter: Why Mocktails?

WHY MOCKTAILS?

Imagine a world where classification of beverages goes beyond whether or not they contain alcohol. Where every drink is crafted with intention, passion, and a deep respect for the art of mixology. Welcome to the domain of mocktails, where every sip is an adventure, not limited by alcoholic content but enriched by creativity and imagination.

Embracing Inclusivity. The beauty of mocktails is their inherent inclusiveness. They welcome everyone to the table. Pregnant women, individuals who refrain from alcohol due to religious or health reasons, or those simply choosing a sober lifestyle—all can partake in the joy of a finely crafted drink. A celebration isn't about the alcohol content in your glass; it's about the shared experience. Mocktails ensure no one misses out.

Health and Wellbeing. Over the past few years, there's been a significant shift towards health and wellness. The beverages we consume play a pivotal role in this. With mocktails, one can enjoy flavorsome concoctions without the concern of alcohol-related calories, potential hangovers, or other adverse effects. Infused with natural fruits, herbs, and spices, many mocktails can also serve as refreshing, nutrient-rich beverages.

Creativity Unleashed. The absence of alcohol in no way diminishes the potential for creativity. On the contrary, it might even enhance it. The world of mocktails is brimming with possibilities—new flavor combinations, innovative presentation techniques, and the joy of crafting something unique. The palette of ingredients is vast, allowing mixologists to experiment, innovate, and surprise.

Responsibly Refreshing. There are times and places where alcohol might not be appropriate. Maybe it's a business lunch, a daytime event, or any occasion where one needs to stay sharp and focused. Mocktails offer sophistication and taste without the alcoholic punch. They fit seamlessly into numerous scenarios, making them a versatile choice for various events.

Economic and Environmental Benefits. Mocktails can often be more economical than their alcoholic counterparts, without compromising on taste or presentation. Moreover, with a focus on fresh and local ingredients, mocktails can be a sustainable choice, reducing the carbon footprint associated with importing exotic alcoholic brands

A New Experience Every Time. With an ever-expanding repertoire of ingredients and techniques available, diving into mocktails is like opening a new chapter of taste with every creation. From the tangy and spicy to the sweet and sour, there's a mocktail for every palate, mood, and occasion.

As we journey deeper into this book, you'll discover that mocktails aren't just about eliminating alcohol. They're about adding experiences, memories, and moments of sheer delight. They're about connecting with oneself and with others, about cherishing the present, and about celebrating life in its myriad flavors and colors.

So, as we raise our glasses to the world of mocktails, let's revel in the joy, artistry, and passion they bring to our lives. Cheers to the endless possibilities and the adventures that await!

QUICK GUIDE TOOLS

Mocktail crafting is an art, and every artist requires the best tools to create a masterpiece. In the world of mocktails, these tools are essential in creating drinks that not only taste divine but also look aesthetically pleasing. Let's dive deeper into the indispensable tools of the trade.

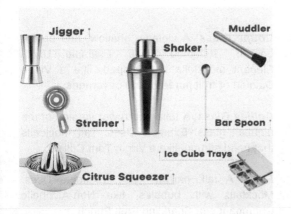

Shaker: The heartbeat of every bartender's toolkit. A shaker ensures that all ingredients meld seamlessly. Its primary purpose is to integrate ingredients smoothly, especially when you have a combination of thick and thin liquids. Shaking gives the drink a crisp, cold temperature and the perfect texture.

Muddler: A muddler is akin to a mortar and pestle for drinks. Used to crush and press ingredients, it's vital for extracting deep flavors from fruits and herbs. When making drinks like mojitos, where the essence of mint is paramount, a muddler is your best friend.

Jigger: The unsung hero of consistency. With its dual-measurement sides, a jigger ensures that you're adding the exact volume of ingredients every single time. This precision is what differentiates a good drink from a great one.

Bar Spoon: More than just a stirring tool, the bar spoon is designed for layered drinks, and its spiral handle assists in creating those beautiful visual gradients in your glass. Plus, with its elongated design, it can reach the bottom of any glass or pitcher.

Citrus Juicer or Squeezer: While bottled juices are handy, nothing beats the freshness of a newly squeezed fruit. This tool ensures maximum juice extraction and leaves behind the seeds and pulp, giving you a pure, vibrant flavor in your mocktails.

Ice Cube Trays: Ice isn't just about cooling your drink. The shape and size of ice cubes can influence dilution and presentation. Specialized trays offer various sizes and shapes, adding another layer of creativity to your concoctions.

Strainer: A strainer is all about presentation and texture. Once you've shaken or stirred your drink to perfection, the strainer ensures that unwanted solid elements (like seeds or herbs) don't find their way into the final pour.

Highball Glass   Coupe Glass   Lowball Glass   Hurricane Glass   Flute Glass

Margarita Glass   Martini Glass   Mule Mug   Punch Bowl & Cups

GLASSWARE

The canvas for your liquid art. Each glass design serves a purpose, influencing aroma, temperature, and even how the drink is sipped. The right glass can elevate even the simplest of mocktails:

Highball Glass: A tall, straight-sided glass, perfect for long drinks. Example Uses: Fizzy mocktails, citrusy coolers, and drinks with a lot of mixers.

Lowball Glass: A short, wide glass, typically used for drinks served "on the rocks." Example Uses: Mocktails with muddled ingredients, like a Virgin Mojito or a No-Alcohol Old Fashioned.

Martini Glass: A stemmed glass with a wide, shallow bowl, perfect for drinks without ice. Example Uses: Classic mocktails that are shaken or stirred and then strained, like a Mocktini.

Coupe Glass: A vintage, shallow, and broad-bowled, stemmed glass. Example Uses: Elegant mocktails best sipped, like a Virgin Daiquiri or fruit purée-based beverages.

Collins Glass: A taller, narrower version of the highball glass. Example Uses: Tall mocktails that need stirring, like a Virgin Tom Collins.

Flute: A tall, narrow glass. Example Uses: Mocktails with bubbles, like Non-Alcoholic Champagne or Sparkling Fruit Punch.

Hurricane Glass: A curvaceous, tall glass with a short stem. Example Uses: Tropical and fruity mocktails, such as a Virgin Piña Colada.

Margarita/Coupette Glass: A stemmed glass with a wide rim, perfect for a salt or sugar edge. Example Uses: Mocktails like a No-Tequila Margarita or drinks that benefit from a rimmed edge.

Choose your perfect glass.

Mule Mug: A copper mug, typically used for Moscow Mules. Example Uses: Mocktails that are served cold and benefit from the insulating property of the mug, like a Virgin Moscow Mule.

Punch Bowl & Cups: A large bowl with matching cups, perfect for serving large quantities. Example Uses: For parties and gatherings, serving drinks like Fruit Punch or a Virgin Sangria.

Tiki Glass: Decorative, often ceramic, and comes in various shapes and sizes. Example Uses: Tropical and exotic mocktails, adding to the thematic experience.

Shot Glass: A small glass suitable for drinks meant to be consumed in one gulp. Example Uses: Miniature versions of mocktails or layered drinks.

Each glass has its own unique character and purpose. Choosing the right glassware can significantly elevate the appearance, aroma, and taste of your mocktail. Ensure your glass complements the drink inside, and you'll always make a lasting impression!

TECHNIQUES

Crafting a perfect mocktail requires the same level of dedication and skill as any alcoholic beverage. With a harmonious blend of ingredients and the right techniques, you can create non-alcoholic drinks that are every bit as intriguing and delightful as their spirited counterparts.

HOW TO SHAKE?

Shaking is a fundamental technique in the world of mixology, particularly vital for achieving a seamless blend of ingredients and the perfect temperature for your cocktail or mocktail. Here's how to master the art of shaking:

Preparation:
- Choose a shaker: The most common types are the Boston shaker and the cobbler shaker.
- Ensure both parts of your shaker are clean and free of any residues.

Add Ingredients:
- Begin by adding your chosen ingredients into the shaker.
- Typically, you'd start with the least expensive ingredients first (like juices or syrups) to ensure if a mistake is made, you can adjust without wasting premium spirits.

Fill with Ice:
- Add ice until the shaker is two-thirds full. Using plenty of ice ensures rapid and even cooling of the mixture.

Seal the Shaker:
- If using a Boston shaker, place the smaller tin on top and tap it to create an airtight seal. With a cobbler shaker, simply place the lid and cap on top.

The Shake:
- Hold the shaker with both hands (one on the top and one on the bottom) and shake vigorously.
- The shake should be powerful and last for about 10-15 seconds. You'll know it's ready when the surface of the shaker feels cold to the touch.

Straining:
- Remove the top of the shaker. If using a Boston shaker, use a strainer to pour the liquid into a glass, keeping the ice in the shaker.
- For cobbler shakers, the built-in strainer will keep the ice at bay.

Serving:
- Once strained, serve the drink immediately in your chosen glassware.

Tip:
Practice makes perfect. The more you shake, the better you'll get at gauging the right intensity and duration for each type of drink. Always remember to shake with a smile – it's part of the fun!

HOW TO MUDDLE?

Muddling is a technique used to extract the essential oils, flavors, and aromas from fresh ingredients, such as fruits, herbs, and spices. This method is the backbone of many classic cocktails and mocktails, ensuring that the flavors meld together seamlessly. Here's a step-by-step guide on how to muddle effectively:

Choose Your Tool:
- While there are specialized tools called muddlers, in a pinch, the back of a spoon can work. A good muddler should be sturdy and easy to grip. They come in various materials like wood, stainless steel, or plastic.

Prepare the Ingredients:
- Wash and clean any fresh ingredients you plan to use. If it's fruit, you may need to slice or segment it. For herbs, plucking the leaves is often enough.

Add Ingredients to Glass or Shaker:
- Place the ingredients you want to muddle at the bottom of the glass or shaker. If you're making a cocktail or mocktail, this is usually done before adding the liquid ingredients.

Muddle with Care:
- Press down on the ingredients using the muddler and give a few gentle twists. The aim is to break down the ingredients just enough to release their flavors – not to pulverize them.
- For herbs like mint, a gentler touch is necessary as over-muddling can make them bitter.

Check Consistency:
- Depending on the ingredient, you might be looking for a puree-like consistency (like with berries) or just a slight bruising (like with mint leaves).

Proceed with the Recipe:
- Once muddled to your satisfaction, continue with the rest of the drink's preparation, whether that's adding ice, other ingredients, or shaking/stirring.

Tip:
Some ingredients take more effort to muddle than others. For instance, muddling sugar with citrus to make a base for a caipirinha or mojito will require a bit more elbow grease than lightly bruising some mint leaves for a mint julep. Always consider the ingredient's nature and the desired end result for your drink.

HOW TO LAYER?

Layering is a technique used to create visually stunning cocktails and mocktails by stacking different ingredients atop one another. The layers are formed based on the specific gravity or density of each liquid, resulting in a stratified look. Here's how you can achieve this technique:

Understand the Densities:
- The success of layering depends on knowing the relative densities of your ingredients. Typically, sugar content, alcohol content, and thickness determine this. For instance, syrups are denser than most juices, which are denser than most liqueurs.

Choose the Right Tool:
- A bar spoon or even a regular teaspoon is essential for this method. It will help you pour the liquids slowly, ensuring they don't mix.

Start with the Densest Liquid:
- Begin by pouring your densest ingredient first. This will be your base layer.

Slowly Pour the Next Layer:
- Hold the spoon upside down with its tip against the inside edge of the glass just above the previous layer.
- Slowly pour the next ingredient over the back of the spoon so that it runs gently down the side of the glass. If done carefully, this liquid will float on top of the previous layer without mixing.

Continue Layering:
- Repeat the above step for each layer, always considering the density of the liquid.

Serve Immediately:
- Layered drinks are best served quickly after preparation to maintain the separation. Instruct the drinker to mix before consuming to ensure they get all the flavors in one sip.

Tip:
- Chilling ingredients can help with layering as cold liquids tend to mix less easily than room temperature ones.
- It might take a few tries to perfect this technique, especially if you're unfamiliar with the densities of the ingredients you're using. Practice makes perfect!

HOW TO RIM GARNISHING?

Rim garnishing adds an aesthetic and flavorful touch to cocktails and mocktails. It's a method that involves coating the rim of the glass with a liquid and then dipping it into a powdered or granulated ingredient, such as salt, sugar, or spices. Here's a step-by-step guide to perfecting the rim garnishing technique:

Prepare the Glass:
- Start with a clean, dry glass. Ensure there's no moisture on the rim as this can interfere with the garnishing process.

Choose Your Binder:
- A binder helps the powdered or granulated ingredient adhere to the glass rim. Common binders include citrus wedges (like lemon or lime), fruit purees, or simple syrup. Determine the binder based on the flavor profile of the drink.

Apply the Binder:
- Cut a notch in your citrus wedge, so it slides onto the rim easily. Run the wedge around the entire circumference of the rim, ensuring it's moistened evenly.
- Alternatively, if using a liquid binder like syrup, dip just the rim into a shallow plate containing the liquid.

Choose Your Garnish:
- Depending on the drink, you can use salt, sugar, crushed candies, grated citrus zest, ground spices, or even finely chopped herbs. Place your chosen garnish on a flat plate in an even layer.

Dip and Rotate:
- Invert the glass and dip the moistened rim into the garnish, rotating it to ensure an even coat. Gently tap the glass to shake off any excess.

Let It Set:
- Once the rim is garnished, let it sit for a minute to allow the garnish to set. This prevents it from dripping or falling off when you pour the drink.

Pour the Drink:
- Carefully pour the prepared drink into the glass, ensuring it doesn't touch or disturb the garnished rim.

Tip:
- For a more pronounced flavor, consider double-dipping: Apply one layer of garnish, let it set, and then repeat the process.
- Use colored sugars or edible glitters for festive occasions or themed parties.

HOW TO GARNISH?

Garnishing is an art that elevates the visual appeal and sensory experience of drinks and dishes. It adds a finishing touch, complements flavors, and can provide a hint about the ingredients within. Here's a comprehensive guide to mastering the art of garnishing:

Preparation:
- Gather all the ingredients you'll need for the garnish.
- Ensure they are fresh, vibrant, and appropriate for the drink or dish.
- Set up a clean workspace with sharp knives, peelers, and other necessary tools.

Selecting Your Garnish:
- The garnish should relate to and enhance the primary elements of the drink or dish. Think about flavors, textures, and colors.
- For cocktails and mocktails, consider citrus slices, fresh herbs, berries, edible flowers, or even spices.

Cutting and Shaping:
- Use sharp knives and peelers to achieve clean cuts.
- Citrus fruits can be sliced, twisted, or even zested.
- Harder fruits and vegetables can be carved into shapes or used as spears or stir sticks.
- Fresh herbs can be slapped between your hands to release their aromatic oils.

Placement:
- Determine where the garnish will be most effective. It can float atop a drink, sit on the rim, dangle off the side, or even stand tall from the center.
- For dishes, consider placing the garnish where it complements the dish's layout and doesn't hide the main ingredients.

Edibility:
- While some garnishes are meant for visual appeal alone, many are intended to be consumed. Ensure that whatever you use is edible and free from pesticides or other chemicals.

Creativity:
- Let your imagination run wild! Explore using unexpected ingredients as garnishes, such as dried fruits, candy, or even small cookies.
- Remember, the goal is to enhance the overall experience of the dish or drink.

Final Touch:
- Once your garnish is placed, give it a final check. Ensure it's secure, especially for drinks, so it doesn't suddenly sink or topple.

Tips:
- Always thoroughly cleanse fruits, vegetables, and herbs before utilizing them as garnishes.
- Keep garnishes refrigerated until the moment you need them to maintain freshness.
- Practice makes perfect! Try various methods and approaches until you discover what works best for you.

CITRUS SYMPHONY SPRITZ

🍸 2 servings 🕐 10 minutes

EQUIPMENT

Cocktail shaker, Citrus juicer or squeezer, Fine mesh strainer, Glassware (Champagne flute or Collins glass)

INGREDIENTS

- 1 oz freshly squeezed orange juice
- 0.5 oz freshly squeezed lemon juice
- 0.5 oz freshly squeezed lime juice
- 0.5 oz grapefruit juice
- 1 oz simple syrup (adjust to taste)
- 2 oz sparkling water or club soda
- Ice cubes
- Orange, lemon, lime, and grapefruit zest for garnish

DIRECTIONS

#1

1. Chill the Glass: Place your chosen glass in the freezer for a few minutes to get a nice chill.
2. Prepare the Citrus Juices: Using the citrus juicer, extract fresh juice from the orange, lemon, lime, and grapefruit.
3. Shake it Up: In the cocktail shaker, combine the freshly squeezed citrus juices, simple syrup, and ice cubes. Shake well until the outside of the shaker is cold.
4. Strain and Pour: Strain the shaken mixture into the chilled glass to remove any pulp or ice shards.
5. Top with Sparkle: Gently top up the glass with sparkling water or club soda, ensuring a good fizz.
6. Garnish: Use a zester or peeler to take thin strips of zest from the citrus fruits. Twist them over the drink to release the oils and then drop them in or place on the rim of the glass.

NUTRITIONAL INFORMATION

90 calories; 12g sugars; 0.5g protein; 20g carbohydrates; 0g fat; 2g fiber; 0mg cholesterol; 10mg sodium; 150mg potassium; Vitamin C: 80% of daily value.

LIME LUMINESCENCE

2 servings   7 minutes

EQUIPMENT

Cocktail shaker, Lime squeezer, Fine mesh strainer, Highball glass.

INGREDIENTS

- 3 oz freshly squeezed lime juice
- 2 oz simple syrup (adjust to taste)
- 1 oz mint syrup (store-bought or homemade)
- 4 oz sparkling water or club soda
- Ice cubes
- Fresh mint leaves for garnish
- Lime wheel for garnish

DIRECTIONS

#2

1. Chill the highball glasses in the freezer for a few minutes.
2. Use the lime squeezer to extract juice from fresh limes.
3. In the cocktail shaker, combine lime juice, simple syrup, mint syrup, and ice cubes. Shake well.
4. Strain the mixture into the chilled highball glasses, ensuring an even divide.
5. Slowly top each glass with sparkling water or club soda to retain effervescence.
6. Garnish with a fresh lime wheel and a sprig of mint.

NUTRITIONAL INFORMATION

85 kcal calories; 16g sugars; 0.2g protein; 20g carbohydrates; 0.1g fat; 0.1g fiber; 0mg cholesterol; 15mg sodium; 60mg potassium; Vitamin C: 25% of daily value.

CITRUS AND SPARKLING CREATIONS

ORANGE OASIS FIZZ

2 servings   **15 minutes**

EQUIPMENT

Juicer, tall glass, stirring spoon.

INGREDIENTS

- Juice of 2 large oranges
- 1 tbsp lemon juice
- 2 tsp agave syrup or honey (optional for added sweetness)
- Sparkling water or club soda
- Ice cubes
- Orange zest and slices for garnish

DIRECTIONS

#3

1. In a juicer, extract the juice from the oranges. This should give you approximately a cup of fresh orange juice.
2. Pour the fresh orange juice into a tall glass.
3. Add the lemon juice and agave syrup or honey to the glass and give it a gentle stir.
4. Add ice cubes to fill the glass to about three-quarters.
5. Slowly top up with sparkling water or club soda, ensuring the effervescence remains.
6. Give the mixture a gentle stir to combine.

NUTRITIONAL INFORMATION

60 calories; 12g sugars; 1g protein; 14g carbohydrates; 0.1g fat; 0.5g fiber; 0mg cholesterol; 10mg sodium; 250mg potassium; Vitamin C: 90% of daily value.

TWILIGHT TANGERINE TONIC

🍸 2 servings

🕐 15 minutes

EQUIPMENT

Cocktail shaker, Juicer, Highball or Collins glass

INGREDIENTS

- 4 fresh tangerines, juiced
- 2 slices of tangerine for garnish
- 1 cup sparkling tonic water
- Crushed ice
- A splash of lime (optional for added zing)
- Mint sprig for garnish (optional)

DIRECTIONS

#4

1. Start by cutting the tangerines in half and using a juicer, extract the juice.
2. In the cocktail shaker, combine the freshly squeezed tangerine juice with a splash of lime (if using).
3. Fill your glass with pulverized ice approximately halfway.
4. Pour the tangerine mixture over the ice until the glass is about two-thirds full.
5. Top off with sparkling tonic water, give it a gentle stir.
6. If desirable, garnish with a tangerine slice and mint sprig.
7. Serve immediately and enjoy the refreshing burst of tangerine with a dash of sparkle.

NUTRITIONAL INFORMATION

220 calories; 24g sugars; 2g protein; 27g carbohydrates; 0g fat; 3g fiber; 0mg cholesterol; 10mg sodium; 340mg potassium; Vitamin C: 80% of daily value.

GRAPEFRUIT GLITTER BURST 2 servings 🕐 7 minutes

EQUIPMENT

Cocktail shaker, Juicer, Highball or Collins glass.

INGREDIENTS

- 2 large fresh grapefruits, juiced
- 2 slices of grapefruit for garnish
- 1 cup carbonated sparkling water
- Crushed ice
- 1 teaspoon of agave syrup or honey (adjust to taste)
- A pinch of salt (optional, to enhance the grapefruit's tartness)
- Rosemary sprig for garnish (optional)

DIRECTIONS

#5

1. Start by cutting the grapefruits in half and using a juicer, extract the juice.
2. In the cocktail shaker, combine the freshly squeezed grapefruit juice, agave syrup or honey, and a pinch of salt (if using). Shake well.
3. Fill your glass with pulverized ice approximately halfway.
4. Pour the grapefruit mixture over the ice until the glass is about two-thirds full.
5. Top off with carbonated sparkling water, give it a gentle stir.
6. If desirable, garnish with a grapefruit slice and a rosemary sprig.
7. Serve immediately and savor the sparkling tang of grapefruit.

NUTRITIONAL INFORMATION

190 calories; 22g sugars; 1g protein; 25g carbohydrates; 0.2g fat; 3g fiber; 0mg cholesterol; 10mg sodium; 300mg potassium; Vitamin C: 95% of daily value.

LEMON LUSTER COOLERSUNRISE CITRUS SODA

2 servings

10 minutes

EQUIPMENT

Cocktail shaker, Juicer, Ice cube tray, Drinking glasses.

INGREDIENTS

- 2 large lemons, juiced
- 1 tablespoon of sugar (or to taste)
- Soda water or sparkling water
- Ice cubes
- Lemon slices for garnish

DIRECTIONS

#6

1. In the cocktail shaker, combine lemon juice and sugar. Shake until sugar is dissolved.
2. Fill glasses with ice cubes.
3. Pour the lemon mixture over the ice, dividing evenly between the glasses.
4. Top up with soda water or sparkling water.
5. Garnish with a lemon slice.

NUTRITIONAL INFORMATION

190 calories; 22g sugars; 1g protein; 25g carbohydrates; 0.2g fat; 3g fiber; 0mg cholesterol; 10mg sodium; 300mg potassium; Vitamin C: 95% of daily value.

Enjoy

BUBBLY BERGAMOT BLISS

🌿 2 servings   🕐 15 minutes

EQUIPMENT

Teapot or kettle, Glass mug or highball glass, Strainer Spoon.

INGREDIENTS

- Two Earl Grey tea sachets or two teaspoons of loose tea
- 1 fresh bergamot or lemon peel for zest
- 1 cup boiling water
- 1 cup sparkling water
- Ice cubes
- Honey or sugar (optional)

DIRECTIONS

#7

1. Boil water and pour over Earl Grey tea in a teapot. Let steep for 4-5 minutes.
2. While tea is steeping, zest the bergamot or lemon peel.
3. Fill a glass mug or highball glass half full with ice cubes.
4. Strain the tea into the glass, filling it half way.
5. Stir in honey or sugar if desired.
6. Top up the glass with sparkling water.
7. Garnish with the bergamot or lemon zest.
8. Stir gently to mix, and serve immediately.

NUTRITIONAL INFORMATION

210 calories; 5g sugars; 1g protein; 50g carbohydrates; 0.1g fat; 2g fiber; 0mg cholesterol; 15mg sodium; 60mg potassium; Vitamin C: 60% of daily value.

CITRUS AND SPARKLING CREATIONS

YUZU SPARKLE SPLASHCLEMENTINE CASCADE

 2 servings   5 minutes

EQUIPMENT

Cocktail shaker, Jigger or measuring tool, Strainer, Highball or similar glasses, Ice cube tray.

INGREDIENTS

- 2 oz Yuzu juice (can be adjusted for tartness)
- 1 oz Simple syrup (optional for added sweetness)
- Soda water or club soda to top up
- Ice cubes
- Yuzu zest or slice for garnish

DIRECTIONS

#8

1. Fill the cocktail shaker with ice cubes.
2. Pour in the yuzu juice and simple syrup (if using).
3. Shake well until the shaker becomes cold to the touch.
4. Strain the mixture into highball glasses filled with ice.
5. Top up with soda water or club soda.
6. Garnish with a slice or zest of yuzu.

NUTRITIONAL INFORMATION

110 calories; 15g sugars; 0g protein; 16g carbohydrates; 0g fat; 0g fiber; 0mg cholesterol; 10mg sodium; 40mg potassium; Vitamin C: 75% of daily value.

CLEMENTINE CASCADE

👐 2 servings   🕐 5 minutes

EQUIPMENT

Citrus juicer, Cocktail shaker, Highball glass.

INGREDIENTS

- 4 ripe clementines
- 1 cup sparkling water
- Ice cubes
- Clementine zest (for garnish)
- Mint leaves (optional, for garnish)

DIRECTIONS

1. Peel the clementines and juice them using the citrus juicer.
2. In the cocktail shaker, combine the clementine juice and ice cubes. Shake well.
3. Fill the highball glass halfway with ice cubes.
4. Pour the shaken clementine juice over the ice.
5. Top with sparkling water until the glass is full.
6. Garnish with a twist of clementine zest and optionally, a mint leaf.

NUTRITIONAL INFORMATION

60 calories; 12g sugars; 1g protein; 15g carbohydrates; 0.1g fat; 2g fiber; 0mg cholesterol; 10mg sodium; 300mg potassium; Vitamin C: 90% of daily value.

ISLAND EUPHORIA

EQUIPMENT

Cocktail shaker, Strainer, Highball glass.

INGREDIENTS

- 2 oz pineapple juice
- 1 oz mango puree
- 1 oz passion fruit juice
- 0.5 oz coconut cream
- 0.5 oz white rum (optional)
- Crushed ice
- Pineapple wedge and maraschino cherry for garnish

DIRECTIONS

#10

1. Fill the cocktail shaker with crushed ice.
2. Add pineapple juice, mango puree, passion fruit juice, coconut cream, and rum to the shaker.
3. Shake vigorously for about 15 seconds.
4. Strain into an ice-filled highball glass.
5. Serve with a pineapple wedge and a maraschino cherry as garnish.

NUTRITIONAL INFORMATION

180 calories; 24g sugars; 1g protein; 35g carbohydrates; 2g fat; 3g fiber; 0mg cholesterol; 5mg sodium; 300mg potassium; Vitamin C: 85% of daily value.

MANGO MOONLIGHT SERENADE

2 servings · 10 minutes

EQUIPMENT

Blender, Fine-mesh strainer, Cocktail shaker, Chilled cocktail glass.

INGREDIENTS

- 1 1/2 ripe mangoes, peeled and pitted
- 2 oz pineapple juice
- 1 oz coconut cream
- 1 oz white rum (optional)
- 1/2 oz fresh lime juice
- Ice cubes
- Sliced mango and a sprig of mint for garnish

DIRECTIONS

#11

1. In a blender, combine the mango, pineapple juice, and coconut cream. Blend until smooth.
2. Pour the mixture through a fine-mesh strainer into a cocktail shaker to remove any pulp.
3. Add rum (if using), lime juice, and ice to the shaker.
4. Shake well until the mixture is chilled.
5. Pour out the cocktail into a chilled cocktail glass.
6. Serve with a piece of mango and a sprig of mint as garnish.
7. Serve immediately and enjoy the tropical bliss.

NUTRITIONAL INFORMATION

210 calories; 28g sugars; 1g protein; 35g carbohydrates; 0.5g fat; 3g fiber; omg cholesterol; 10mg sodium; 320mg potassium; Vitamin C: 100% of daily value.

PALM BEACH PASSION PUNCH

👥 2 servings   🕐 10 minutes

EQUIPMENT

Cocktail shaker, measuring jigger, tall glass, strainer.

INGREDIENTS

- 4 oz passionfruit juice
- 2 oz coconut milk
- 1 oz white rum (optional)
- 1 oz lime juice
- Ice cubes
- Passionfruit seeds and coconut flakes for garnish

DIRECTIONS

#12

1. Combine passionfruit juice, coconut milk, rum (if using), and lime juice in a cocktail shaker.
2. Shake rapidly until the fluid is cold, filling the shaker halfway with ice cubes.
3. Pour out into a large glass half-filled with ice.
4. Garnish with passion fruit seeds and coconut flakes.
5. Serve immediately and enjoy the tropical vibes!

NUTRITIONAL INFORMATION

250 calories; 30g sugars; 2g protein; 35g carbohydrates; 5g fat; 3g fiber; 0mg cholesterol; 15mg sodium; 400mg potassium; Vitamin C: 80% of daily value.

EQUIPMENT

Cocktail shaker, Fine mesh strainer, Tall glass, Ice cube tray.

INGREDIENTS

- 2 hibiscus tea bags
- 4 oz boiling water
- 2 oz pineapple juice
- 1 oz coconut milk
- 1 oz light rum (optional)
- 1/2 oz lime juice
- 1/2 oz agave nectar or honey
- Ice cubes
- Pineapple slices and hibiscus petals for garnish

DIRECTIONS

#13

1. Start by steeping the hibiscus tea bags in boiling water for about 5 minutes. Once steeped, remove the tea bags and let the tea cool.
2. In the cocktail shaker, combine the cooled hibiscus tea, pineapple juice, coconut milk, rum (if using), lime juice, and agave nectar.
3. Fill the shaker halfway with ice and aggressively shake for 15 seconds.
4. Strain the concoction into a tall glass filled with ice.
5. Add a pineapple segment and a few hibiscus petals as garnish.

NUTRITIONAL INFORMATION

150 calories; 18g sugars; 0.5g protein; 20g carbohydrates; 2g fat; 0.3g fiber; 0mg cholesterol; 10mg sodium; 250mg potassium; Vitamin C: 50% of daily value.

PINEAPPLE PALMS PARADISE

🍴 2 servings   🕐 10 minutes

EQUIPMENT

Blender, Tall glass, Cocktail stirrer or spoon, Measuring cup.

INGREDIENTS

- 1 cup fresh pineapple chunks
- 2 cups pineapple juice
- 1/4 cup coconut cream
- Ice cubes
- Pineapple slice and coconut flakes for garnish

DIRECTIONS

#14

1. In a blender, combine the fresh pineapple chunks, pineapple juice, and coconut cream.
2. Blend until smooth and creamy.
3. Fill the tall glass half full with ice cubes.
4. Pour the blended mixture over the ice.
5. Stir well using the cocktail stirrer or spoon.
6. Top with a slice of pineapple and coconut flakes.

NUTRITIONAL INFORMATION

210 calories; 30g sugars; 1g protein; 40g carbohydrates; 3g fat; 2g fiber; 0mg cholesterol; 10mg sodium; 250mg potassium; Vitamin C: 90% of daily value.

Enjoy

LAGOON LYCHEE LUSH

2 servings   10 minutes

EQUIPMENT

Blender, Strainer, Tall glass,
Measuring cup, Ice cube tray.

INGREDIENTS

- 1 cup fresh lychee, pitted
- 1/2 cup mixed tropical fruits (like passionfruit, guava, and mango), chopped
- 1/4 cup fresh lime juice
- 2 cups crushed ice
- 1 1/2 cups club soda or sparkling water
- Fresh mint leaves for garnish (optional)
- Lychee and tropical fruit slices for garnish

DIRECTIONS

#15

1. In a blender, combine the fresh lychee, mixed tropical fruits, and lime juice. Blend until smooth.
2. Over a large bowl or jug, use a strainer to filter out any seeds or large chunks. Discard the solids.
3. Pour the blended fruit mixture back into the blender and add the crushed ice. Blend again until it achieves a smooth, slushy consistency.
4. Divide the slushy mixture among four tall glasses, filling each about halfway.
5. Top up each glass with sparkling water or club soda, gently stirring to mix.
6. Garnish with a slice of lychee, tropical fruit slices, and optionally, a sprig of fresh mint.
7. Serve immediately and enjoy the tropical sensations!

NUTRITIONAL INFORMATION

75 calories; 14g sugars; 0.4g protein; 18g carbohydrates; 0.2g fat; 1g fiber; 0mg cholesterol; 10mg sodium; 200mg potassium; Vitamin C: 100% of daily value.

SUNSET GUAVA GLIDE

🥤 2 servings 🕐 10 minutes

EQUIPMENT

Cocktail shaker, Muddler, Fine strainer, Tall glass.

INGREDIENTS

- 4 ripe guavas, peeled and deseeded
- 1 lime, juiced
- 2 tsp honey or agave syrup (adjust to taste)
- 4 oz white rum (optional for a non-alcoholic version)
- A handful of fresh mint leaves
- Sparkling water or club soda
- Ice cubes
- Add a lime slice and some mint to the dish as a garnish.

DIRECTIONS

#16

1. In a cocktail shaker, muddle the guava fruit, mint leaves, lime juice, and honey together until the guava releases its juices.
2. Add the white rum (if using) and a handful of ice cubes. Shake vigorously.
3. Ensure that no guava seeds or substantial pulp fragments are transferred by performing a double strain of the mixture into a tall glass filled with ice.
4. Top up with sparkling water or club soda.
5. Gently stir to combine the ingredients.
6. Add a lime slice and some mint to the dish as a garnish.

NUTRITIONAL INFORMATION

175 calories; 20g sugars; 1g protein; 25g carbohydrates; 0.2g fat; 3g fiber; 0mg cholesterol; 5mg sodium; 280mg potassium; Vitamin C: 240% of daily value.

BALI BANANA BLISS

2 servings   10 minutes

EQUIPMENT

Blender, Glass, Knife.

INGREDIENTS

- Ingredients:
- 2 ripe bananas
- 1 cup of pineapple juice
- ½ cup of coconut milk
- 1 tsp of honey (optional for added sweetness)
- A handful of ice cubes
- A slice of lime for garnish
- A sprinkle of toasted coconut for garnish

DIRECTIONS

#17

1. In the blender, combine the bananas, pineapple juice, coconut milk, and honey.
2. Blend until smooth and creamy.
3. Pulse momentarily again after adding a handful of ice cubes.
4. Pour the mixture into glasses.
5. Garnish with a slice of lime and a sprinkle of toasted coconut.
6. Serve immediately and enjoy the tropical bliss!

NUTRITIONAL INFORMATION

280 calories; 32g sugars; 2g protein; 45g carbohydrates; 12g fat; 3g fiber; 0mg cholesterol; 15mg sodium; 500mg potassium; Vitamin C: 75% of daily value.

CORAL COVE COCONUT COOLER

🍸 2 servings   🕐 10 minutes

EQUIPMENT

Blender, Strainer, Tall glass, Ice cube tray.

INGREDIENTS

- 1 cup coconut milk (full-fat)
- ½ cup pineapple juice
- ¼ cup mango juice
- 2 tsp lime juice
- 1 tsp honey or agave syrup (adjust to taste)
- Ice cubes
- Coconut flakes for garnish
- Pineapple wedge for garnish

DIRECTIONS

#18

1. In the blender, combine coconut milk, pineapple juice, mango juice, lime juice, and honey or agave syrup.
2. Blend until smooth and creamy.
3. Fill a tall glass halfway with ice cubes.
4. Pour the blended mixture over the ice.
5. Garnish with a sprinkle of coconut flakes and a pineapple wedge on the rim.
6. Serve immediately and enjoy the tropical vibes.

NUTRITIONAL INFORMATION

180 calories; 15g sugars; 1g protein; 22g carbohydrates; 10g fat; 3g fiber; 0mg cholesterol; 10mg sodium; 250mg potassium; Vitamin C: 70% of daily value.

Enjoy

TAHITIAN TROPIC TWIRL

🧑‍🍳 2 servings 🕐 10 minutes

EQUIPMENT

Cocktail shaker, Tall glass, Measuring jigger, Strainer, Knife for slicing.

INGREDIENTS

- 1.5 oz light rum
- 1 oz coconut milk
- 2 oz fresh mango juice
- 1 oz passionfruit pulp
- 0.5 oz lime juice
- Crushed ice
- Mango and passionfruit slices for garnish
- For a fragrant touch, add a sprig of mint.

DIRECTIONS   #19

1. In a cocktail shaker, combine light rum, coconut milk, mango juice, passionfruit pulp, and lime juice. Shake vigorously until the mixture is chilled.
2. Fill a tall glass with crushed ice.
3. Strain and pour the cocktail mixture over the ice, filling the glass.
4. Garnish with slices of mango and passionfruit, letting them float atop the drink.
5. Place the sprig of mint as a finishing touch.
6. Serve immediately.

NUTRITIONAL INFORMATION

200 calories; 14g sugars; 1g protein; 18g carbohydrates; 1g fat; 2g fiber; 0mg cholesterol; 10mg sodium; 250mg potassium; Vitamin C: 40% of daily value.

BERRY BALLET BLISS

🍴 2 servings   🕐 10 minutes

EQUIPMENT

Blender, Fine mesh strainer, Glassware (Preferably a tall glass).

INGREDIENTS

- 1 cup mixed berries (blueberries, raspberries, strawberries, blackberries)
- 2 cups sparkling water or club soda
- 1 tablespoon honey (adjust based on sweetness preference)
- Ice cubes
- Mint leaves for garnish (optional)

DIRECTIONS

#20

1. Place the mixed berries and honey in the blender and blend until smooth.
2. Remove any seeds from the blended mixture by straining it through a fine mesh strainer into a jug.
3. Fill the glasses with ice cubes.
4. Pour the berry mixture equally into the glasses.
5. Top up with sparkling water or club soda.
6. Stir gently using a bar spoon.
7. If desirable, add a mint sprig as a garnish.
8. Enjoy the refreshing flavor of assorted berries upon serving.

NUTRITIONAL INFORMATION

85 calories; 14g sugars; 1g protein; 20g carbohydrates; 0.5g fat; 4g fiber; 0mg cholesterol; 10mg sodium; 120mg potassium; Vitamin C: 60% of daily value.

STRAWBERRY SUNBURST SMOOTHIE

2 servings   10 minutes

EQUIPMENT

Blender, Measuring cups and spoons, Tall serving glass, Straw (optional).

INGREDIENTS

- 2 cups fresh strawberries, hulled and halved
- 1 ripe banana, peeled and sliced
- 1/2 cup fresh pineapple chunks
- 1/2 cup fresh mango chunks
- 1 cup coconut water or almond milk
- 1 tbsp agave nectar (optional, for extra sweetness) or honey
- Ice cubes (optional, for a colder drink)

DIRECTIONS

#21

1. In a blender, combine strawberries, banana, pineapple, mango, and coconut water or almond milk.
2. Blend on high until the mixture is smooth and creamy.
3. Taste and, if desired, add honey or agave nectar to sweeten further. Blend again to mix.
4. If a colder smoothie is preferred, add ice cubes and blend until smooth.
5. Pour out the smoothie into serving glasses and serve immediately.
6. Serving Recommendations:
7. On the rim of the glass, a slice of pineapple or garnish with a fresh strawberry.
8. Perfect for breakfast or a midday refreshment.

NUTRITIONAL INFORMATION

160 calories; 30g sugars; 2g protein; 40g carbohydrates; 0.5g fat; 5g fiber; 0mg cholesterol; 70mg sodium; 600mg potassium; Vitamin C: 180% of daily value.

BERRY BALLET BLISS

👐 2 servings   🕐 5 minutes

EQUIPMENT

Blender, Strainer, Glass (preferably a tall glass).

INGREDIENTS

- 1 cup fresh blueberries
- 1/2 cup almond milk for a dairy-free option or plain yogurt
- 1/2 cup crushed ice
- 1 tablespoon maple syrup or honey
- A splash of vanilla extract
- Mint leaves for garnish (optional)

DIRECTIONS

#22

1. In the blender, combine blueberries, yogurt or almond milk, crushed ice, honey (if using), and vanilla extract.
2. Blend until the mixture is smooth. If the mixture is too thick, thin it up with a little water or additional almond milk.
3. Using a strainer, pour the mix into glasses to remove any leftover blueberry skins.
4. Garnish with fresh mint leaves if desired.
5. Serve immediately and enjoy the soothing flavors of the Blueberry Breeze Bay.

NUTRITIONAL INFORMATION

110 calories; 14g sugars; 3g protein; 17g carbohydrates; 2.5g fat; 2g fiber; 7mg cholesterol; 40mg sodium; 150mg potassium; Vitamin C: 15% of daily value.

RASPBERRY ROSE REVERIE

🌿 2 servings   🕐 10 minutes

EQUIPMENT

Blender, Fine mesh strainer, Glassware of choice.

INGREDIENTS

- 1 cup fresh raspberries
- 1.5 cups cold water
- 2 tablespoons rose water
- 1 tablespoon honey (or adjust to taste)
- 2 teaspoons freshly squeezed lemon juice
- Ice cubes
- Fresh rose petals for garnish (ensure they are edible and pesticide-free)
- A small sprig of mint (optional for garnish)

DIRECTIONS

1. In a blender, combine raspberries, water, rose water, honey, and lemon juice. Blend until smooth.
2. Pour the mixture through a fine-mesh strainer into a pitcher, pressing with a spoon to extract as much liquid as possible.
3. Discard the seeds and pulp.
4. Fill glasses with ice cubes.
5. Pour the raspberry-rose mixture over the ice.
6. Garnish with a few fresh rose petals and optionally, a sprig of mint.
7. Stir gently and serve immediately.
8. Serving Recommendations: Best enjoyed on a warm day or as a sophisticated non-alcoholic option for evening gatherings. Pair with light pastries or finger foods.

NUTRITIONAL INFORMATION

60 calories; 10g sugars; 0.5g protein; 14g carbohydrates; 0.2g fat; 3g fiber; 0mg cholesterol; 5mg sodium; 90mg potassium; Vitamin C: 30% of daily value.

FRUITFUL FOREST FUSION

  2 servings   🕐 10 minutes

EQUIPMENT

Blender, Fine mesh strainer, Tall glass.

INGREDIENTS

- 1/2 cup wild blueberries
- 1/2 cup raspberries
- 1/4 cup blackberries
- 1/4 cup strawberries, hulled and halved
- 1 ripe kiwi, peeled and sliced
- 1/2 ripe banana
- 1/4 cup pomegranate seeds
- 1 cup apple juice (unsweetened)
- 1/2 cup orange juice
- 1 tbsp honey or agave nectar (optional)
- A handful of ice cubes

DIRECTIONS

#24

1. In the blender, combine all the berries, kiwi, banana, and pomegranate seeds.
2. Pour in the apple and orange juice.
3. Add agave nectar or honey if you prefer a sweeter taste.
4. Blend until the mixture is smooth.
5. Blend until the mixture is smooth. If the mixture is too thick, thin it up with a little water or additional almond milk.
6. Pour out the strained mixture into tall glasses filled with ice cubes.
7. Garnish with a few berries on top or a slice of kiwi on the rim.

NUTRITIONAL INFORMATION

160 calories; 32g sugars; 2g protein; 40g carbohydrates; 1g fat; 5g fiber; 0mg cholesterol; 10mg sodium; 450mg potassium; Vitamin C: 120% of daily value.

BERRIES AND FRUIT MIXES

CHERRY CHERRY TWILIGHT TWIST

🍸 2 servings   🕐 5 minutes

EQUIPMENT

Blender, Glassware: Tall glass, Citrus squeezer.

INGREDIENTS

- 1 cup of sweet cherries, pitted
- 1/2 cup of tart cherries, pitted
- Juice of half a lemon
- Juice of half an orange
- 1 cup of crushed ice
- 1 tablespoon of agave syrup or honey
- Mint leaves for garnish (optional)
- Orange or lemon slice for garnish

DIRECTIONS

#25

1. In a blender, combine the sweet cherries, tart cherries, lemon juice, and orange juice.
2. If desired, add honey or agave syrup for an additional touch of sweetness.
3. Blend in the crushed ice until smooth.
4. Taste and adjust sweetness if needed.
5. Pour into glasses, garnishing with a slice of orange or lemon and a mint leaf.
6. Serve immediately and enjoy the delightful twist of cherries and citrus.

NUTRITIONAL INFORMATION

110calories; 25g sugars; 1g protein; 28g carbohydrates; 0.2g fat; 2g fiber; 0mg cholesterol; 3mg sodium; 320mg potassium; Vitamin C; 50% of daily value.

BLACKBERRY BRAMBLE BLISS

🥤 2 servings 🕐 10 minutes

EQUIPMENT

Blender or cocktail shaker, Fine mesh strainer, Tall serving glass.

INGREDIENTS

- 1 cup fresh blackberries, plus a few extra for garnish
- 2 teaspoons sugar or honey (adjust to taste)
- Juice of 1/2 lemon
- 1 cup sparkling water or tonic water
- Crushed ice

Enjoy

DIRECTIONS

#26

1. In a blender or using a muddler in a bowl, crush the blackberries until they release their juice.
2. Add the honey or sugar and lemon juice, and stir or blend until well combined.
3. Remove the seeds from the mélange by straining it through a fine-mesh strainer into a pitcher.
4. Fill two glasses with crushed ice.
5. Pour the blackberry mixture over the ice, filling each glass half full.
6. Top up each glass with sparkling or tonic water, and give a gentle stir.
7. Garnish with a few whole blackberries on top.

NUTRITIONAL INFORMATION

60 calories; 9g sugars; 1g protein; 15g carbohydrates; 0.5g fat; 4g fiber; 0mg cholesterol; 5mg sodium; 90mg potassium; Vitamin C: 35% of daily value.

BERRIES AND FRUIT MIXES

PEACHY PLUM PIZZAZZ

🌿 2 servings   🕐 10 minutes

EQUIPMENT

Blender, Knife, Cutting board, Serving glass.

INGREDIENTS

- 2 ripe peaches, pitted and sliced
- 3 ripe plums, pitted and sliced
- 1 cup of coconut water or cold water
- 1 tablespoon honey or agave syrup (adjust according to taste)
- Ice cubes (optional)
- Fresh mint leaves for garnish

DIRECTIONS

1. Prepare the fruits by washing them thoroughly. Pit and slice both the peaches and plums.
2. In a blender, add the sliced peaches, plums, cold water or coconut water, and honey or agave syrup.
3. Blend until smooth. If you prefer a colder beverage, add ice cubes and blend again until you reach the desired consistency.
4. Pour the mixture into serving glasses.
5. If desirable, add a mint sprig as a garnish.

NUTRITIONAL INFORMATION

120 calories; 25g sugars; 2g protein; 30g carbohydrates; 0.5g fat; 4g fiber; 0mg cholesterol; 5mg sodium; 450mg potassium; Vitamin C: 25% of daily value.

Enjoy

KIWI BERRY KISS

2 servings   10 minutes

EQUIPMENT

Blender, Measuring cups, Drinking glass.

INGREDIENTS

- 2 ripe kiwis, peeled and sliced
- 1 cup mixed berries (strawberries, blueberries, raspberries)
- 1/2 cup plain yogurt
- 1 tablespoon honey or agave nectar (adjust to taste)
- A handful of ice cubes
- Fresh mint leaves for garnish (optional)

Enjoy

DIRECTIONS

#28

1. Start by placing the sliced kiwis and mixed berries into the blender.
2. Add the yogurt (or almond milk) and honey.
3. Toss in the ice cubes.
4. Blend on high until the mixture is smooth and creamy.
5. Taste and adjust sweetness, if necessary.
6. Pour into glasses, garnish with a mint leaf or a slice of kiwi, and serve immediately.

NUTRITIONAL INFORMATION

150 calories; 22g sugars; 4g protein; 30g carbohydrates; 1g fat; 5g fiber; 3mg cholesterol; 30mg sodium; 400mg potassium; Vitamin C: 150% of daily value.

CRIMSON CURRANT CASCADE

🍹 2 servings   🕐 10 minutes

EQUIPMENT

Blender, Fine strainer, Tall serving glass, Ice cube tray.

INGREDIENTS

- 1 cup fresh red currants, washed and de-stemmed
- 1 ½ cups sparkling water, chilled
- 2 tablespoons honey or agave nectar (adjust to taste)
- 1 teaspoon freshly squeezed lemon juice
- Ice cubes

DIRECTIONS

#29

1. In the blender, combine red currants, honey (or agave nectar), and lemon juice. Blend until smooth.
2. Strain the mixture to remove seeds and any residue, pouring the liquid back into the blender.
3. Add chilled sparkling water and give it a quick blend to mix well.
4. Add a few ice crystals to serving glasses, then pour the Crimson Currant Cascade over the ice.
5. Garnish with a sprig of mint or a few fresh currants on top if desired.

NUTRITIONAL INFORMATION

70 calories; 14g sugars; 0.6g protein; 17g carbohydrates; 0.2g fat; 2g fiber; 0mg cholesterol; 15mg sodium; 270mg potassium; Vitamin C: 50% of daily value.

BERRIES AND FRUIT MIXES

MINT MIRAGE MEDLEY

👐 2 servings 🕐 10 minutes

EQUIPMENT

Blender, Strainer, Tall glass, Muddler.

INGREDIENTS

- 20 fresh mint leaves
- 5 fresh basil leaves
- 5 fresh cilantro leaves
- 1 tablespoon honey (or to taste)
- 2 cups of cold water
- Ice cubes
- Lemon or lime wedges for garnish (optional)

DIRECTIONS #30

1. In a blender, combine the mint, basil, cilantro, and half of the water.
2. Blend until the herbs are finely chopped.
3. In a tall glass, muddle the honey with a few mint leaves to release the flavor.
4. Fill the glass with ice.
5. Pour the blended herb mixture through a strainer into the glass, pressing as hard as possible to extract as much liquid as possible.
6. Add the remaining cold water and give it a quick stir.
7. Garnish with a lime wedge or lemon, if desired.

NUTRITIONAL INFORMATION

40 calories; 9g sugars; 1g protein; 10g carbohydrates; 0g fat; 2g fiber; 0mg cholesterol; 10mg sodium; 50mg potassium; Vitamin C: 15% of daily value.

CHAMOMILE CLOUD CALM

🍵 2 servings   🕐 10 minutes

EQUIPMENT

Kettle or stove, Teapot or heatproof pitcher, Measuring spoons, Knife for slicing.

INGREDIENTS

- 2 chamomile tea bags
- 1 cup of hot water
- 1 tsp honey (optional for sweetness)
- 2 slices of apple (Honeycrisp or Fuji variety)
- 1 slice of orange
- A sprinkle of dried blueberries
- A dash of vanilla extract

DIRECTIONS   #31

1. Utilize a kettle or a stovetop to bring water to a simmer.
2. Place chamomile tea bags in a teapot or heatproof pitcher.
3. Add apple and orange slices along with the dried blueberries.
4. Pour hot water over ingredients in the pot or pitcher.
5. Allow tea to steep for 5 minutes.
6. Remove tea bags and discard.
7. Add vanilla extract and stir.
8. Sweeten with honey if desired.

NUTRITIONAL INFORMATION

25 calories; 4g sugars; 0g protein; 6g carbohydrates; 0g fat; 1g fiber; 0mg cholesterol; 5mg sodium; 55mg potassium; Vitamin C: 20% of daily value.

LAVENDER LULLABY ELIXIR

EQUIPMENT

Teapot or kettle, Tea strainer or infuser, Drinking glass or mug.

INGREDIENTS

- 1 tbsp dried culinary lavender buds
- 2 cups of water
- 2 tsp honey (adjust to taste)
- 1 slice of lemon
- A pinch of edible dried rose petals (optional)

DIRECTIONS

#32

1. Bring two glasses of water to a boil in a teapot or kettle.
2. Place the dried lavender buds in a tea strainer or infuser.
3. Once the water has boiled, pour it over the lavender in the tea strainer or infuser into a glass or mug.
4. Allow the lavender to steep for 5 minutes.
5. Remove the tea strainer or infuser.
6. Stir in honey to sweeten as per your preference.
7. Garnish with a slice of lemon and a sprinkle of edible dried rose petals if desired.
8. Enjoy the calming notes of the Lavender Lullaby Elixir.

NUTRITIONAL INFORMATION

20 calories; 4g sugars; 0g protein; 5g carbohydrates; 0g fat; 0g fiber; 0mg cholesterol; 5mg sodium; 10mg potassium; Vitamin C: 10% of daily value.

Enjoy

GREEN TEA ZEN GARDEN

2 servings   8 minutes

EQUIPMENT

Tea kettle or pot, Tea infuser or tea bag, 2 teacups.

INGREDIENTS

- 2 teaspoons of high-quality green tea leaves or 2 green tea bags
- 2 cups of freshly boiled water
- 1 slice of lemon
- Honey or agave syrup (optional, to taste)

DIRECTIONS

#33

1. In a kettle or pot, bring two glasses of water to a boil.
2. Place the green tea leaves into a tea infuser or directly into a teapot. If using tea bags, simply place them in the teapot.
3. Pour out the boiling water over the tea leaves or tea bags and allow them to infuse for two to three minutes. The steeping time can be adjusted depending on your desired strength.
4. While the tea steeps, squeeze a bit of lemon juice into each teacup.
5. Pour the steeped tea into the teacups, ensuring each has an equal amount of liquid.
6. Sweeten with agave syrup or honey if desired.

NUTRITIONAL INFORMATION

2 calories; 0.2g sugars; 0g protein; 0.3g carbohydrates; 0gfat; 0g fiber; 0mg cholesterol; 9mg sodium; 18mg potassium; Vitamin C: 10% of daily value.

ROSEMARY RADIANCE REFRESHER

 2 servings   10 minutes

EQUIPMENT

Cocktail shaker, Muddler, Fine mesh strainer, Ice cube tray, Tall glass.

INGREDIENTS

- 2 fresh rosemary sprigs, plus additional for garnish
- 1 large lemon, juiced
- 2 teaspoons honey (or to taste)
- 1 cup sparkling water
- Ice cubes

DIRECTIONS

#34

1. In the cocktail shaker, muddle one sprig of rosemary to release its aromatic oils.
2. Add honey and freshly strained lemon juice to the shaker.
3. Shake the shaker aggressively until all of the ingredients are blended.
4. Pour out the ingredients into a tall glass halfway filled with ice..
5. Top off with sparkling water and give it a gentle stir.
6. Garnish with a sprig of rosemary and a slice of lemon.

NUTRITIONAL INFORMATION

40 calories; 9g sugars; 0g protein; 10g carbohydrates; 0g fat; 0.5g fiber; 0mg cholesterol; 5mg sodium; 60mg potassium; Vitamin C: 45% of daily value.

Enjoy

HIBISCUS HAVEN HARMONY

👥 2 servings   🕐 10 minutes

EQUIPMENT

Teapot or saucepan, Strainer, Stirring spoon, Glass or mug.

INGREDIENTS

- 2 hibiscus tea bags or 2 tablespoons dried hibiscus petals
- 2 cups of water
- 1 tablespoon honey or agave nectar (adjust to taste)
- 1/2 cup tropical fruit juice (pineapple, mango, or passion fruit recommended)
- Ice cubes
- Fresh tropical fruit slices (for garnish)
- Mint leaves (optional, for garnish)

DIRECTIONS   #35

1. Boil the water in a teapot or saucepan.
2. Add the hibiscus tea bags or dried petals to the boiling water.
3. Allow 4-5 minutes for the tea to steep.
4. Take remove the tea bags or filter the petals.
5. Incorporate the honey or agave nectar until totally dissolved.
6. Allow the tea to cool for a few minutes, then mix in the tropical fruit juice.
7. Pour out the hibiscus mixture over ice cubes in glasses.
8. Garnish with fresh tropical fruit slices and optionally, a sprig of mint.

NUTRITIONAL INFORMATION

50 calories; 8g sugars; 0g protein; 12g carbohydrates; 0g fat; 0g fiber; 0mg cholesterol; 5mg sodium; 50mg potassium; Vitamin C: 40% of daily value.

LEMON VERBENA VERVE

2 servings · 5 minutes

EQUIPMENT

Cocktail shaker or stirring rod, Fine mesh strainer, Glass (preferably chilled)

INGREDIENTS

- 1 handful of fresh lemon verbena leaves (or 2 tea bags of dried lemon verbena)
- 1 cup of cold water
- 1/2 cup mixed fresh berries (like raspberries, blueberries, and strawberries)
- 2 teaspoons honey or agave syrup (adjust to taste)
- Ice cubes
- Lemon slices and berries for garnish

DIRECTIONS

#36

1. If using fresh lemon verbena, gently muddle the leaves at the base of the shaker to release the oils. If using tea bags, steep in cold water for about 15 minutes.
2. Add the fresh berries to the shaker and gently muddle to release their juices.
3. Fill the shaker with ice cubes.
4. Pour the cold water and honey/agave syrup into the shaker.
5. Shake vigorously for about 15 seconds.
6. Strain the mixture into the chilled glass.
7. Garnish with a lemon slice and a few berries.

NUTRITIONAL INFORMATION

45 calories; 8g sugars; 0.5g protein; 11g carbohydrates; 0.2g fat; 2g fiber; 0mg cholesterol; 2mg sodium; 55mg potassium; Vitamin C: 25% of daily value.

EARL GREY EUPHORIA ESCAPE

2 servings   8 minutes

EQUIPMENT

Teapot or kettle, Teacup, Teaspoon.

INGREDIENTS

- 1 Earl Grey tea bag or 1 teaspoon of loose Earl Grey tea
- 1 cup of boiling water
- 1-2 teaspoons of honey (adjust to taste)

DIRECTIONS

#37

1. Boil water using a kettle or on the stove.
2. Place the Earl Grey tea bag or loose tea into the teacup.
3. Pour the boiling water into the cup, ensuring the tea is fully submerged.
4. Steep the tea for 3-5 minutes, depending on your preference for strength.
5. Remove the tea bag or strain the loose tea.
6. Add honey, stirring until fully dissolved.
7. Sip and enjoy the aromatic blend of Earl Grey with the sweet undertones of honey.

NUTRITIONAL INFORMATION

22 calories; 5g sugars; 0g protein; 6g carbohydrates; 0g fat; 0g fiber; 0mg cholesterol; 7mg sodium; 18mg potassium; Vitamin C: 0% of daily value.

JASMINE JEWEL JOY

🫗 2 servings   🕐 9 minutes

EQUIPMENT

Teapot or brewing vessel, Tea strainer or infuser, Teacup or glass mug, Spoon.

INGREDIENTS

- 2 teaspoons of jasmine tea leaves
- 2 cups of freshly boiled water
- 1 fresh peach, thinly sliced
- Optional: Honey or sweetener of choice

DIRECTIONS

#38

1. Allow water to cool somewhat once it has been brought to a boil.
2. Place jasmine tea leaves in the teapot or infuser.
3. Pour out the boiled water over the tea leaves and steep for 3-4 minutes.
4. Add peach slices to the teapot and allow them to infuse for an additional minute.
5. Strain the tea into cups and, if desired, sweeten with honey or preferred sweetener.
6. Garnish with an additional peach slice if desired.

NUTRITIONAL INFORMATION

30 calories; 4g sugars; 0g protein; 7g carbohydrates; 0g fat; 1g fiber; 0mg cholesterol; 10mg sodium; 140mg potassium; Vitamin C: 8% of daily value.

ROOIBOS RED RHAPSODY

2 servings | 10 minutes

EQUIPMENT

Teapot or kettle, Teacup, Citrus squeezer (optional)

INGREDIENTS

- 2 teaspoons of rooibos tea leaves (or 2 tea bags)
- 2 cups of boiling water
- 1 medium-sized orange (for zest and juice)
- Optional: Sweetener of choice (honey, agave, etc.)

DIRECTIONS

#39

1. Bring the water to a boil in a kettle or teapot.
2. Place the rooibos tea leaves or tea bags in the teapot or directly in teacups.
3. Pour the boiling water over the tea and let steep for 5 minutes.
4. While the tea is steeping, zest the orange using a fine grater, ensuring not to include the bitter white pith. Set aside a pinch of zest for garnish.
5. Squeeze the juice from half of the orange.
6. Remove the tea leaves or tea bags after the tea has brewed.
7. Stir in the orange juice and, if preferred, the sweetener.
8. Garnish each cup with a sprinkle of orange zest.

NUTRITIONAL INFORMATION

15 calories; 2g sugars; og protein; 4g carbohydrates; og fat; 1g fiber; omg cholesterol; 10mg sodium; 70mg potassium; Vitamin C: 45% of daily value.

VELVET VANILLA VOYAGE

🍸 2 servings   🕐 15 minutes

EQUIPMENT

Saucepan, Whisk, Measuring spoons, Glass or mug.

INGREDIENTS

- 2 cups of whole milk
- 2 tsp of high-quality vanilla extract
- 1 tbsp of caramel sauce, plus extra for drizzling
- Whipped cream (optional)

DIRECTIONS

1. Warm but not boiling milk in a saucepan over medium heat.
2. Reduce the heat to low and add the vanilla extract and caramel sauce.
3. Continuously whisk until all of the ingredients are well incorporated and the mixture is smooth.
4. Pour out the drink into two glasses or mugs.
5. If desirable, top the pudding with whipped cream and drizzle with more.
6. Serving Recommendations: Serve warm, ideally paired with shortbread cookies or a slice of buttery pound cake.

NUTRITIONAL INFORMATION

180 calories; 20g sugars; 6g protein; 24g carbohydrates; 7g fat; 0g fiber; 20mg cholesterol; 95mg sodium; 250mg potassium; Vitamin C: 0% of daily value.

CREAMY AND DESSERT MOCKTAILS

CHOCOLATE CHIFFON CHARM

2 servings   10 minutes

EQUIPMENT

Saucepan, Whisk, Serving mug or glass.

INGREDIENTS

- 2 cups of milk
- 3 tablespoons of high-quality cocoa powder
- 2 tablespoons of sugar (adjust to taste)
- 1 teaspoon of vanilla extract
- Whipped cream (for topping)
- Chocolate shavings or cocoa powder (for garnish)

DIRECTIONS

#41

1. Milk, cocoa powder, and sugar should be combined in a saucepan. Heat over medium flame while whisking continuously until the mixture is smooth and well-combined.
2. Remove the dish from the flame and stir in the vanilla extract.
3. Pour out the chocolate mixture into serving mugs or glasses.
4. Add a generous amount of whipping cream to each portion.
5. Decorate the drink with chocolate morsels or cocoa powder.

NUTRITIONAL INFORMATION

220 calories; 24g sugars; 8g protein; 35g carbohydrates; 7gfat; 2g fiber; 20mg cholesterol; 105mg sodium; 320mg potassium; Vitamin C: 0% of daily value.

TIRAMISU TWILIGHT TEMPTATION

🥄 2 servings   🕐 15 minutes

EQUIPMENT

Blender, Saucepan, Whisk, Serving glass or mug.

INGREDIENTS

- 2 cups of brewed coffee, cooled
- ½ cup of mascarpone cheese
- 1 teaspoon of vanilla extract
- 2 tablespoons of cocoa powder
- 3 tablespoons of sugar
- Whipped cream for garnish
- Ladyfingers or savoiardi biscuits - 2 (optional for serving)
- Cocoa powder or chocolate shavings for garnish

DIRECTIONS

#42

1. In a blender, combine the brewed coffee, mascarpone cheese, vanilla extract, cocoa powder, and sugar. Blend until smooth.
2. In a saucepan, heat the ingredients over medium heat until heated but not boiling. Stir occasionally.
3. Pour the mixture into serving glasses or mugs.
4. Top with a dollop of whipped cream.
5. Finish with a sprinkling of cocoa powder or chocolate shavings.
6. Serve with a ladyfinger on the side if desired.

NUTRITIONAL INFORMATION

350 calories; 28g sugars; 8g protein; 40g carbohydrates; 15gfat; 1g fiber; 40mg cholesterol; 90mg sodium; 150mg potassium; Vitamin C: 2% of daily value.

BANOFFEE BLISSFUL BURST

👥 2 servings   🕐 15 minutes

EQUIPMENT

Blender, Saucepan, Whisk, Glass.

INGREDIENTS

- 2 ripe bananas, sliced
- 2 cups milk (or almond milk for a dairy-free alternative)
- 2 tbsp toffee sauce, plus extra for drizzling
- 1 tbsp sugar (optional)
- Whipped cream for topping
- A pinch of salt
- Crushed graham crackers or biscuits (optional, for garnish)

DIRECTIONS

#43

1. Warm the milk over medium heat in a saucepan until it begins to simmer. Do not let it boil.
2. Add sliced bananas, toffee sauce, sugar, and a pinch of salt to the blender.
3. Pour the steaming milk over the banana-toffee mixture in the blender.
4. Blend until smooth and creamy.
5. Pour the mixture into glasses.
6. Top with a generous amount of whipped cream.
7. Drizzle extra toffee sauce over the whipped cream.
8. Optionally, sprinkle some crushed graham crackers or biscuits on top for an added crunch.

NUTRITIONAL INFORMATION

320 calories; 38g sugars; 6g protein; 52g carbohydrates; 8g fat; 2g fiber; 25mg cholesterol; 130mg sodium; 480mg potassium; Vitamin C: 10% of daily value.

CREAMY AND DESSERT MOCKTAILS

CARAMEL CLOUD CAROUSEL

🥄 2 servings   🕐 15 minutes

EQUIPMENT

: Saucepan, Whisk, Measuring spoons, Glasses for serving.

INGREDIENTS

- Caramel sauce: 4 tbsp (plus extra for garnish)
- Whole milk: 2 cups
- Heavy cream: 4 tbsp
- Vanilla extract: 1/2 tsp
- Sea salt: A pinch (optional)

DIRECTIONS

#44

1. In a saucepan, combine whole milk, caramel sauce, and a pinch of sea salt. The mixture should be heated over medium heat until it is hot but not boiling.
2. Incorporate the heavy cream and vanilla extract into a mixing bowl.
3. Once the desired temperature has been reached, remove from flame and pour into glasses.
4. Drizzle with additional caramel sauce for garnish.

NUTRITIONAL INFORMATION

350 calories; 42g sugars; 6g protein; 44g carbohydrates; 18g fat; 0g fiber; 60mg cholesterol; 240mg sodium; 290mg potassium; Vitamin C: 0% of daily value.

Enjoy

CREAMY AND DESSERT MOCKTAILS

COCONUT CREAM CASCADE

🖐 2 servings   🕐 5 minutes

EQUIPMENT

: Blender, Tall glass, Measuring cup, Stirrer.

INGREDIENTS

- 1 cup coconut cream
- 1/2 cup fresh pineapple juice
- 1/4 cup pineapple chunks
- 2 tablespoons shredded coconut (for garnish)
- Ice cubes
- Pineapple wedge (for garnish)

DIRECTIONS

#45

1. In a blender, combine the coconut cream, fresh pineapple juice, and pineapple chunks.
2. Blend until smooth.
3. Fill a tall glass half-way with ice cubes.
4. Pour the blended mixture over the ice.
5. Garnish with shredded coconut on top.
6. Place a pineapple wedge on the rim of the glass for added aesthetics.
7. Stir gently before sipping and enjoy the tropical flavors.

NUTRITIONAL INFORMATION

280 calories; 12g sugars; 2g protein; 18g carbohydrates; 22g fat; 2g fiber; 0mg cholesterol; 15mg sodium; 250mg potassium; Vitamin C: 60% of daily value.

MOCHA MOONLIGHT MUSE

🍸 2 servings   🕐 10 minutes

EQUIPMENT

Coffee maker or espresso machine, Milk frother (optional), Saucepan, Whisk, Coffee mug or glass.

INGREDIENTS

- 2 cups freshly brewed coffee or 2 shots of espresso
- 1 cup whole milk
- 2 tbsp cocoa powder
- 2 tbsp sugar (adjust to taste)
- 2 oz dark chocolate, finely chopped
- Whipped cream for garnish (optional)

Enjoy

DIRECTIONS

#46

1. Brew your coffee or espresso and keep it hot.
2. Cocoa powder, milk, and sugar are combined in a saucepan. Whisk until the mixture is smooth.
3. Stir the milk mixture over medium heat until it is heated but not scalding, stirring constantly.
4. Stir in the coarsely chopped dark chocolate until completely melted and blended.
5. Pour the brewed coffee or espresso into your mug or glass.
6. Pour in the chocolate milk mixture slowly, stirring gently to incorporate.
7. If desired, top with whipped cream.

NUTRITIONAL INFORMATION

230 calories; 24g sugars; 6g protein; 35g carbohydrates; 9g fat; 2g fiber; 15mg cholesterol; 105mg sodium; 390mg potassium; Vitamin C: 0.5% of daily value.

STRAWBERRIES & CREAM SERENADE

2 servings   10 minutes

EQUIPMENT

Blender, Bowl, Spoon, Serving glass.

INGREDIENTS

- Fresh ripe strawberries: 1 cup, hulled and halved
- Heavy cream: 1/2 cup
- Granulated sugar or honey: 2 tablespoons (adjust to taste)
- Crushed ice: 1/2 cup
- Mint leaves (optional): for garnish

DIRECTIONS

#47

1. In the blender, combine strawberries, heavy cream, sugar or honey, and crushed ice.
2. Mix until a uniform and creamy consistency is reached.
3. Taste and adjust sweetness, if needed.
4. Pour into serving glasses.
5. Garnish with a strawberry slice or a mint leaf on top, if desired.
6. Serve immediately and enjoy the symphony of flavors.

NUTRITIONAL INFORMATION

220 calories; 15g sugars; 2g protein; 20g carbohydrates; 12g fat; 2g fiber; 50mg cholesterol; 20mg sodium; 210mg potassium; Vitamin C: 80% of daily value.

Enjoy

PISTACHIO PUDDING PARADISE

🖐 4 servings   🕐 25 minutes

EQUIPMENT

Medium saucepan, Whisk, Mixing bowl, Serving bowls.

INGREDIENTS

- 2 cups whole milk
- 1/2 cup granulated sugar
- 1/4 cup unsalted pistachios, finely ground
- 1/4 cup cornstarch
- 1/2 tsp vanilla extract
- A pinch of salt
- Whole pistachios and whipped cream for garnish (optional)

DIRECTIONS

#48

1. In a medium saucepan, combine milk, sugar, ground pistachios, and salt. Continuous stirring while heating over medium heat until the sugar dissolved.
2. In a separate basin, combine 3 tablespoons of cold water with cornstarch to form a smooth paste. Slowly whisk this into the heated milk mixture.
3. Whisking continuously, continue heating the mixture over medium heat until it reaches pudding consistency.
4. Add vanilla extract and remove from heat.
5. Transfer the pudding to serving bowls and let it cool. Refrigerate for at least 2 hours before serving.
6. Before serving, garnish with whole pistachios and a dollop of whipped cream, if desired.

NUTRITIONAL INFORMATION

230 calories; 28g sugars; 5g protein; 35g carbohydrates; 8g fat; 1g fiber; 12mg cholesterol; 60mg sodium; 230mg potassium; Vitamin C: 2% of daily value.

LEMON MERINGUE LULLABY

🍸 2 servings   🕐 15 minutes

EQUIPMENT

Medium saucepan, Whisk, Measuring cups and spoons, Blender.

INGREDIENTS

- 1 cup whole milk
- 2 tablespoons lemon curd
- 1 teaspoon lemon zest
- 2 tablespoons sugar
- 2 tablespoons whipped cream
- 1/2 teaspoon pure vanilla extract
- A pinch of salt
- Crushed graham crackers for garnish
- Meringue pieces for garnish

DIRECTIONS

#49

1. In a saucepan, combine milk, lemon curd, lemon zest, and sugar.
2. Heat on medium, whisking continuously until the sugar dissolves and the mixture is well-combined.
3. Once heated, remove from stove and let it cool for a few minutes.
4. Pour the mixture into a blender, add vanilla extract and a pinch of salt. Blend until smooth.
5. Pour into serving glasses, top with a dollop of whipped cream.
6. Garnish with crushed graham crackers and meringue pieces.
7. Serve immediately and enjoy the creamy tangy delight.

NUTRITIONAL INFORMATION

180 calories; 20g sugars; 4g protein; 22g carbohydrates; 8g fat; 0g fiber; 25mg cholesterol; 85mg sodium; 150mg potassium; Vitamin C: 8% of daily value.

CRYSTAL CLEAR COSMO

🥤 2 servings   🕐 5 minutes

EQUIPMENT

Cocktail shaker, Fine strainer, Martini glass, Jigger or measuring tool, Ice cube tray.

INGREDIENTS

- 4 oz cranberry juice (unsweetened)
- 1 oz fresh lime juice
- 1 oz simple syrup (adjust to taste)
- Soda water or club soda for topping up
- Ice cubes
- Lime twist or wedge for garnish

DIRECTIONS   #50

1. Fill the cocktail shaker with ice cubes.
2. Add cranberry juice, fresh lime juice, and simple syrup to the shaker.
3. Shake well until the outside of the shaker feels chilled.
4. Fine strain the mixture into a chilled martini glass.
5. Top up with soda water or club soda to achieve the desired level.
6. Garnish with a lime twist or wedge.

NUTRITIONAL INFORMATION

65 calories; 14g sugars; 0.2g protein; 16g carbohydrates; 0g fat; 0.1g fiber; 0mg cholesterol; 5mg sodium; 30mg potassium; Vitamin C: 25% of daily value.

NO-GIN GARDEN TONIC

EQUIPMENT

Cocktail shaker, Tall glass (highball), Muddler, Ice cubes.

INGREDIENTS

- 1 oz elderflower cordial
- 1 oz fresh cucumber juice
- 1/2 oz fresh lime juice
- 3 fresh basil leaves
- 1 sprig rosemary
- Tonic water (to top off)
- Cucumber slice and rosemary sprig (for garnish)

DIRECTIONS

#51

1. In the cocktail shaker, muddle basil leaves and rosemary sprig.
2. Add elderflower cordial, cucumber juice, and lime juice.
3. Shake well until the mixture is chilled.
4. Strain into an ice-filled highball glass.
5. Top off with tonic water.
6. Cucumber and rosemary sprigs serve as garnishes.

NUTRITIONAL INFORMATION

75 calories; 14g sugars; 0g protein; 18g carbohydrates; 0g fat; 0.2g fiber; 10mg cholesterol; 10mg sodium; 45mg potassium; Vitamin C: 8% of daily value.

VIRGIN MARY'S MORNING

🍸 1 servings   🕐 8 minutes

EQUIPMENT

Cocktail shaker, Large glass (highball or tumbler), Ice cubes, Stirring stick.

INGREDIENTS

- 4 oz tomato juice
- 1 oz fresh lemon juice
- 1/2 oz Worcestershire sauce
- 2 dashes of hot sauce (adjust to taste)
- Pinch of celery salt
- Pinch of ground black pepper
- Pinch of smoked paprika
- 1 celery stalk (for garnish)
- 1 lemon wedge (for garnish)
- Pickled green bean or olive

DIRECTIONS   #52

1. In the cocktail shaker, combine tomato juice, lemon juice, Worcestershire sauce, hot sauce, celery salt, black pepper, and smoked paprika.
2. Shake well until the mixture is well-blended.
3. Fill a highball or tumbler glass with ice cubes.
4. Pour the shaken mixture over the ice.
5. Stir gently with the stirring stick.
6. If desirable, garnish with a pickled green bean or olive.

NUTRITIONAL INFORMATION

35 calories; 6g sugars; 1g protein; 9g carbohydrates; 0g fat; 1g fiber; 0mg cholesterol; 370mg sodium; 300mg potassium; Vitamin C: 70% of daily value.

CLASSIC MOCKTAILS MADE SIMPLE

PIÑA COOL-ADA

EQUIPMENT

Blender, Tall glass (preferably a hurricane or highball glass), Ice cube tray, Pineapple leaf (for garnish).

INGREDIENTS

- 1 cup fresh pineapple chunks
- 1/2 cup coconut milk (full fat for creaminess)
- 1/4 cup coconut cream
- 1/2 teaspoon vanilla extract
- 1 tablespoon honey or agave syrup (adjust to taste)
- 1 cup ice cubes
- Pineapple slice and cherry (for garnish)

Enjoy

DIRECTIONS

#53

1. In the blender, combine the fresh pineapple chunks, coconut milk, coconut cream, vanilla extract, and sweetener.
2. Blend on high until smooth.
3. Add ice crystals and continue blending until the mixture is smooth and chilled.
4. Pour the Piña Cool-ada into the tall glass.
5. Garnish with a pineapple slice, cherry, and a leaf from the pineapple if available.

NUTRITIONAL INFORMATION

280 calories; 22g sugars; 2g protein; 32g carbohydrates; 14g fat; 3g fiber; 0mg cholesterol; 20mg sodium; 325mg potassium; Vitamin C: 80% of daily value.

SUNRISE SANS TEQUILA

EQUIPMENT

Tall glass (highball), Stirrer, Ice cubes.

INGREDIENTS

- 4 oz orange juice, freshly squeezed
- 2 oz pomegranate juice (or grenadine for sweeter taste)
- 1/2 oz fresh lemon juice
- 1/2 oz simple syrup (optional for added sweetness)
- Orange slice and maraschino cherry for garnish
- Sparkling water or soda water (optional, for effervescence)

DIRECTIONS

#54

1. Fill the highball glass with ice cubes.
2. Pour out in the orange juice until the glass is about three-quarters full.
3. If using, add fresh lemon juice and simple syrup. Stir gently.
4. Slowly pour the pomegranate juice or grenadine over the back of a spoon, letting it settle at the bottom of the glass to create a gradient effect.
5. Optionally, top with a splash of sparkling water or soda water for a fizzy touch.
6. Orange slice on the rim and a maraschino cherry in the cocktail are the appropriate garnishes.

NUTRITIONAL INFORMATION

120 calories; 25g sugars; 1g protein; 28g carbohydrates; 0.2g fat; 0.5g fiber; 0mg cholesterol; 10mg sodium; 325mg potassium; Vitamin C: 90% of daily value.

MOJITO MIRAGE

EQUIPMENT

Cocktail shaker, Muddler, Tall glass (highball), Ice cubes.

INGREDIENTS

- 10 mint leaves, plus one mint stem for garnish
- 1/2 lime, cut into 4 wedges
- 2 tablespoons white sugar, or to taste
- 1 cup ice cubes
- 1/2 cup soda water or club soda
- 1 oz fresh lime juice
- Lime wheel and mint sprig, for garnish

DIRECTIONS   #55

1. In a robust glass, combine mint leaves and one lime wedge. Using the muddler, muddle the mint and lime to release the mint oils and lime liquid.
2. Add two additional lime wedges and sugar, and muddle again to extract additional lime juice. Avoid straining the mélange.
3. Fill the glass almost to the top with ice cubes. Pour the fresh lime juice over the ice.
4. Top off with soda water or club soda.
5. Stir well to mix the ingredients. Taste and adjust sugar if desired.
6. Decorate with a lime wheel and a mint twig.

NUTRITIONAL INFORMATION

70 calories; 16g sugars; 0g protein; 17g carbohydrates; 0g fat; 0.5g fiber; 0mg cholesterol; 25mg sodium; 225mg potassium; Vitamin C: 25% of daily value.

NO-RUM DAIQUIRI DREAM

🍸 1 servings   🕐 6 minutes

EQUIPMENT

Cocktail shaker, Strainer, Chilled cocktail or martini glass, Ice cubes.

INGREDIENTS

- 1 1/2 oz fresh lime juice
- 1 oz simple syrup (adjust to taste)
- 1/2 oz fresh orange juice (for added depth)
- Splash of soda water or lemon-lime soda (optional, for effervescence)
- Lime wheel or zest (for garnish)

DIRECTIONS   #56

1. In the cocktail shaker, combine fresh lime juice, simple syrup, and fresh orange juice with ice.
2. Shake vigorously until the exterior of the shaker feels icy.
3. In a chilled cocktail or martini flute, strain the mixture.
4. Add a splash of carbonated water or lemon-lime soda, if desired, for a minor fizz.
5. Garnish with a lime wheel or a strip of lime zest.

NUTRITIONAL INFORMATION

90 calories; 14g sugars; 0g protein; 15g carbohydrates; 0g fat; 0.5g fiber; 0mg cholesterol; 20mg sodium; 255mg potassium; Vitamin C: 25% of daily value.

WHISKEYLESS SOUR

1 servings   6 minutes

EQUIPMENT

Cocktail shaker, Ice cubes, Old-fashioned glass.

INGREDIENTS

- 1 1/2 oz fresh lemon juice
- 3/4 oz simple syrup (adjust to taste)
- 1/4 oz almond orgeat syrup (for a hint of nutty flavor)
- 1/2 oz aquafaba (chickpea water; acts as a substitute for egg white for frothiness)
- A few dashes of aromatic bitters (optional for added depth)
- Maraschino cherry and orange slice (for garnish)

DIRECTIONS

#57

1. In the cocktail shaker, combine lemon juice, simple syrup, almond orgeat syrup, and aquafaba.
2. Shake vigorously for about 15-20 seconds to create a nice froth from the aquafaba.
3. The mixture should be strained into an old-fashioned glass full with ice.
4. If using, add a few dashes of aromatic bitters on top.
5. As a garnish, include a maraschino cherry and an orange segment.

NUTRITIONAL INFORMATION

60 calories; 12g sugars; 0g protein; 14g carbohydrates; 0g fat; 0.1g fiber; 0mg cholesterol; 5mg sodium; 255mg potassium; Vitamin C: 20% of daily value.

MIMOSA MUSE

🍸 1 servings   🕐 3 minutes

EQUIPMENT

Champagne flute.

INGREDIENTS

- 3 oz non-alcoholic sparkling wine or club soda
- 3 oz freshly squeezed orange juice (preferably cold)
- Orange twist or slice for garnish

DIRECTIONS

#58

1. Ensure both the non-alcoholic sparkling wine (or club soda) and orange juice are chilled.
2. Fill the champagne flute halfway with the freshly squeezed orange juice.
3. Slowly top off with the non-alcoholic sparkling wine or club soda, being careful to avoid excessive fizzing.
4. Gently stir to combine, ensuring not to break the effervescence.
5. Orange segment or slice may be used as a garnish.

NUTRITIONAL INFORMATION

60 calories; 12g sugars; 1g protein; 13g carbohydrates; 0g fat; 0.2g fiber; 5mg cholesterol; 5mg sodium; 250mg potassium; Vitamin C: 100% of daily value.

CUBAN LIBRE CAREFREE

1 servings · 3 minutes

EQUIPMENT

Tall glass (highball), Ice cubes, Stirring spoon.

INGREDIENTS

- 8 oz cola (regular or diet, according to preference)
- Juice of 1/2 fresh lime
- Lime wheel or wedge (for garnish)

DIRECTIONS   #59

1. Fill a highball glass with ice cubes.
2. Squeeze the juice of half a lime over the ice.
3. Pour the cola over the lime juice and ice, filling the glass.
4. Gently stir to mix the lime juice and cola together.
5. A lime wheel or wedge should be placed on the rim of the glass.

NUTRITIONAL INFORMATION

110 calories; 27g sugars; 0g protein; 33g carbohydrates; 0g fat; 0.2g fiber; 5mg cholesterol; 10mg sodium; 150mg potassium; Vitamin C: 0% of daily value.

Enjoy

SAPPHIRE SODA SOIREE

🥤 1 servings   🕐 6 minutes

EQUIPMENT

Tall glass, Muddler, Ice cubes, Strainer.

INGREDIENTS

- 10 fresh blueberries
- 5 fresh mint leaves
- 1 oz freshly squeezed lemon juice
- 2 tsp agave syrup or honey (adjust to taste)
- Sparkling soda water (to top off)
- Additional blueberries and a mint sprig (for garnish)

DIRECTIONS

#60

1. In the bottom of the glass, muddle the blueberries and mint leaves together until the blueberries release their juice and the mint is fragrant.
2. Add the lemon juice and agave syrup or honey, and mix well.
3. Fill the glass with ice cubes.
4. Top off with sparkling soda water, and give it a gentle stir to mix.
5. Add a few fresh blueberries and a mint sprig to the top of the beverage.
6. Serve immediately with a straw.

NUTRITIONAL INFORMATION

60 calories; 14g sugars; 0.1g protein; 15g carbohydrates; 0.1g fat; 0.5g fiber; 10mg cholesterol; 10mg sodium; 60mg potassium; Vitamin C: 55% of daily value.

FIZZING PEACH FANTASY

🍸 2 servings   🕐 6 minutes

EQUIPMENT

Tall glass (highball), Cocktail stirrer, Ice cubes.

INGREDIENTS

- 4 oz peach nectar
- 8 oz sparkling water
- 1 fresh peach, sliced for garnish

DIRECTIONS

1. Fill an old-fashioned glass with ice crystals halfway.
2. Pour in the peach nectar.
3. Slowly add the sparkling water, allowing the fizz to rise.
4. Gently stir using the cocktail stirrer.
5. Garnish with a fresh peach slice.

Enjoy

NUTRITIONAL INFORMATION

45 calories; 12g sugars; 0.5g protein; 13g carbohydrates; 0.1g fat; 1g fiber; 10mg cholesterol; 10mg sodium; 150mg potassium; Vitamin C: 8% of daily value.

CITRUS CYCLONE SPARKLER

🥂 2 servings   🕐 8 minutes

EQUIPMENT

Tall glass (highball), Cocktail stirrer, Juicer.

INGREDIENTS

- 2 oz fresh orange juice
- 2 oz fresh lemon juice
- 1 oz fresh lime juice
- 1 oz fresh grapefruit juice
- 8 oz soda water
- Citrus slices (orange, lemon, lime, grapefruit) for garnish

Enjoy

DIRECTIONS

#62

1. Using a juicer, extract fresh juices from the citrus fruits.
2. In an ice-filled highball glass, combine the freshly squeezed orange, lemon, lime, and grapefruit juices.
3. Top off with soda water, filling the glass.
4. Gently stir using the cocktail stirrer to mix the ingredients.
5. Garnish with slices of citrus fruits.

NUTRITIONAL INFORMATION

60 calories; 10g sugars; 0.6g protein; 15g carbohydrates; 0.1g fat; 1g fiber; 0mg cholesterol; 20mg sodium; 200mg potassium; Vitamin C: 90% of daily value.

RASPBERRY RADIANCE RISER

🥄 2 servings   🕐 6 minutes

EQUIPMENT

Tall glass (highball), Cocktail stirrer, Ice cubes.

INGREDIENTS

- 5 oz raspberry puree
- 7 oz soda water
- 1 oz lemon juice
- Fresh raspberries and a lemon slice for garnish

DIRECTIONS

#63

1. Place ice cubes into the highball glass, filling it halfway.
2. Add the raspberry puree into the glass.
3. Pour in the lemon juice for that tangy kick.
4. Slowly introduce the soda water, causing a playful fizz.
5. Stir gently with the cocktail stirrer to mix well.
6. Serve with fresh raspberries and a lemon slice on the rim of the glass.

NUTRITIONAL INFORMATION

60 calories; 14g sugars; 0.3g protein; 15g carbohydrates; 0.1g fat; 2g fiber; 0mg cholesterol; 10mg sodium; 45mg potassium; Vitamin C: 15% of daily value.

Enjoy

GOLDEN GINGER GALE

2 servings • 10 minutes

EQUIPMENT

Tall glass (highball), Cocktail stirrer, Ice cubes.

INGREDIENTS

- 4 oz fresh ginger juice
- 2 tsp honey (adjust to taste)
- 8 oz soda water
- 1 oz lime juice
- Lime slices and crystallized ginger for garnish

DIRECTIONS

#64

1. In the glass, combine ginger juice and honey, stirring well until the honey is fully dissolved.
2. Fill the glass halfway with ice cubes.
3. Pour in the soda water, followed by the lime juice.
4. Stir gently using the cocktail stirrer to mix.
5. Garnish with a slice of lime and a piece of crystallized ginger on the rim.

NUTRITIONAL INFORMATION

50 calories; 12g sugars; 0.4g protein; 13g carbohydrates; 0.1g fat; 0.2g fiber; 0mg cholesterol; 10mg sodium; 40mg potassium; Vitamin C: 10% of daily value.

Enjoy

TROPICAL TORNADO TWIST

👐 2 servings   🕐 10 minutes

EQUIPMENT

Tall glass (highball), Cocktail stirrer, Ice cubes.

INGREDIENTS

- 3 oz pineapple juice
- 2 oz mango puree
- 2 oz passionfruit juice
- 6 oz sparkling water
- Slices of pineapple, mango, and passionfruit for garnish

DIRECTIONS

#65

1. Half-fill a highball glass with ice cubes.
2. Pour in the pineapple juice, mango puree, and passionfruit juice.
3. Slowly add the sparkling water, letting the tropical fusion come alive with bubbles.
4. Gently stir the mixture using the cocktail stirrer.
5. Garnish with slices of pineapple, mango, and passionfruit.

NUTRITIONAL INFORMATION

80 calories; 18g sugars; 0.5g protein; 20g carbohydrates; 0.1g fat; 2g fiber; 0mg cholesterol; 10mg sodium; 210mg potassium; Vitamin C: 70% of daily value.

Enjoy

LAVENDER LUMINANCE LIFT

🌱 2 servings   🕐 8 minutes

EQUIPMENT

Tall glass (highball), Cocktail stirrer, Ice cubes, Zester or grater.

INGREDIENTS

- 2 teaspoons dried culinary lavender
- 10 oz soda water
- 1 tablespoon simple syrup or agave nectar (adjust to taste)
- Zest of 1 lemon
- Lemon slices, for garnish

DIRECTIONS

#66

1. In the bottom of the glass, muddle the dried lavender gently to release its oils.
2. Add ice cubes to fill the glass halfway.
3. Pour out in the simple syrup or agave nectar.
4. Slowly pour soda water, allowing the effervescence to activate the lavender aroma.
5. Zest the lemon directly into the glass for a burst of citrusy brightness.
6. Gently stir using the cocktail stirrer.
7. Garnish with a slim lemon slice.

NUTRITIONAL INFORMATION

30 calories; 7g sugars; 0g protein; 8g carbohydrates; 0g fat; 0g fiber; 0mg cholesterol; 10mg sodium; 20mg potassium; Vitamin C: 10% of daily value.

CHERRY CHARM CHILLER

2 servings   6 minutes

EQUIPMENT

Tall glass (highball), Cocktail stirrer, Ice cubes.

INGREDIENTS

- 5 oz cherry juice
- 7 oz soda water
- 1 tsp vanilla extract
- Fresh cherries for garnish
- 1 scoop of crushed ice

DIRECTIONS

#67

1. In the tall glass, add the crushed ice.
2. Pour in the cherry juice over the ice.
3. Add the vanilla extract.
4. Slowly top up with soda water, allowing for a fizzy reaction.
5. Stir gently using the cocktail stirrer.
6. Garnish with a fresh cherry on the rim.

NUTRITIONAL INFORMATION

50 calories; 10g sugars; 0.2g protein; 12g carbohydrates; 0.1g fat; 0.5g fiber; 0mg cholesterol; 15mg sodium; 100mg potassium; Vitamin C: 5% of daily value.

Enjoy

PINEAPPLE PIZZAZZ POP

🤟 2 servings   🕐 6 minutes

EQUIPMENT

Tall glass (highball), Cocktail stirrer, Ice cubes.

INGREDIENTS

- 5 oz pineapple juice
- 7 oz soda water
- 1 lime, half-squeezed for juice and half sliced for garnish

DIRECTIONS

#68

1. Fill a highball glass with ice cubes up to the halfway mark.
2. Pour in the pineapple juice over the ice.
3. Squeeze in the lime juice and gently mix.
4. Slowly add the soda water, letting the bubbles gently merge with the juice.
5. Garnish with a thin lime slice.

NUTRITIONAL INFORMATION

60 calories; 14g sugars; 0.5g protein; 15g carbohydrates; 0.1g fat; 0.5g fiber; 0mg cholesterol; 5mg sodium; 120mg potassium; Vitamin C: 12% of daily value.

Enjoy

MYSTICAL MINTY MIRAGE

2 servings   8 minutes

EQUIPMENT

Tall glass (highball), Cocktail stirrer, Ice cubes.

INGREDIENTS

- 10 fresh mint leaves
- 4 oz cucumber juice
- 1 tsp sugar or honey
- 8 oz soda water

DIRECTIONS

#69

1. In the bottom of the glass, muddle the mint leaves with sugar or honey.
2. Fill the glass with ice crystals halfway.
3. Pour in the cucumber juice.
4. Slowly top up with soda water, allowing the bubbles to mingle.
5. Gently stir using the cocktail stirrer.
6. Garnish with a piece of cucumber and a sprig of mint.

NUTRITIONAL INFORMATION

40 calories; 8g sugars; 0.2g protein; 10g carbohydrates; 0.1g fat; 0.5g fiber; 0mg cholesterol; 5mg sodium; 80mg potassium; Vitamin A: 4% of daily value.

WINTER'S WHISPER WARMER

2 servings   15 minutes

EQUIPMENT

Saucepan, Ladle, Mug, Cinnamon stick (for stirring).

INGREDIENTS

- 8 oz apple cider
- 1 cinnamon stick
- 4 whole cloves
- Optional: Slice of apple for garnish

DIRECTIONS

#70

1. In a saucepan, combine apple cider, cinnamon stick, and cloves.
2. Allow the spices to soak for 5 minutes over medium heat.
3. Take the cinnamon stick and cloves from the fire and set aside.
4. Pour the spiced apple cider into mugs.
5. Optional: Garnish with a slice of apple and an additional cinnamon stick for stirring.

NUTRITIONAL INFORMATION

90 calories; 22g sugars; 0g protein; 23g carbohydrates; 0g fat; 0g fiber; 0mg cholesterol; 5mg sodium; 150mg potassium; Vitamin C: 10% of daily value.

Enjoy

SPRING BLOSSOM BLISS

2 servings   8 minutes

EQUIPMENT

Tall glass (highball), Cocktail stirrer, Ice cubes.

INGREDIENTS

- 4 oz floral-infused syrup (e.g., elderflower or rose)
- 8 oz sparkling water or soda
- 1 lemon, zest and juice
- Edible flower petals for garnish (like hibiscus or violets)
- 1 orange slice for garnish

DIRECTIONS

#71

1. Fill a tall glass with ice cubes about halfway.
2. Pour in the floral-infused syrup.
3. Mix in the lemon zest and juice.
4. Gently pour in the sparkling water or soda, creating a fizzy blend.
5. Stir gently using the cocktail stirrer.
6. Garnish with an orange slice and sprinkle edible flower petals on top.

NUTRITIONAL INFORMATION

70 calories, 17g sugars, 0g protein, 18g carbohydrates, 0g fat, 0g fiber, 0mg cholesterol, 5mg sodium, 35mg potassium, Vitamin C: 10% of daily value.

Enjoy

SUMMER SOLSTICE SPLASH

🦋 2 servings 🕐 10 minutes

EQUIPMENT

Blender, Pitcher, Strainer.

INGREDIENTS

- 2 cups Fresh watermelon (cubed)
- 10-12 Fresh mint leaves
- 1 cup Sparkling water
- 1 cup Ice cubes
- 1 Lime (sliced for garnish)
- 1 tablespoon Sugar (optional)

DIRECTIONS

#72

1. Blend the fresh watermelon cubes until smooth in a blender. Add sugar if desired and blend again.
2. Strain the watermelon juice into a pitcher, discarding seeds or pulp.
3. Muddle the mint leaves in the pitcher.
4. Add the ice cubes.
5. Mix in the sparkling water.
6. Serve in glassware with lime slices and a mint sprig garnish.

NUTRITIONAL INFORMATION

120 calories; 18g sugars; 1g protein; 30g carbohydrates; 0.5g fat; 1g fiber; 0mg cholesterol; 20mg sodium; 250mg potassium; Vitamin C: 25% of daily value.

Enjoy

AUTUMN AMBER AMBIANCE

🥄 4 servings   🕐 16 minutes

EQUIPMENT

Blender, Saucepan, Measuring spoons and cups.

INGREDIENTS

- 2 cups pumpkin puree
- 4 cups milk (or almond milk for a dairy-free option)
- 2 tsp ground ginger
- 1 tsp ground nutmeg
- 4 tbsp maple syrup
- 1 tsp vanilla extract
- Whipped cream (optional for garnish)
- A sprinkle of cinnamon (for garnish)

DIRECTIONS

#73

1. Warm the milk in a saucepan over medium heat without allowing it to simmer.
2. Add the pumpkin puree, ginger, nutmeg, maple syrup, and vanilla extract. Stir until fully combined.
3. Remove the mélange from the fire when it reaches the desired temperature.
4. Pour out the mixture into a blender and blend until smooth.
5. Provide in glasses. If desirable, garnish with whipped cream and a dash of cinnamon.

NUTRITIONAL INFORMATION

250 calories; 20g sugars; 7g protein; 38g carbohydrates; 4g fat; 5g fiber; 20mg cholesterol; 105mg sodium; 450mg potassium; Vitamin C: 6% of daily value.

SNOWY SPRUCE SPRITZER

🍸 2 servings   🕙 10 minutes

EQUIPMENT

Highball or stemless wine glasses, Cocktail stirrer or spoon, Measuring cup.

INGREDIENTS

- 16 oz sparkling water
- 2 oz pine needle syrup
- 1 oz cranberry juice
- Fresh cranberries for garnish
- A sprig of fresh pine or spruce for garnish
- Ice cubes

DIRECTIONS

#74

1. Fill each glass with ice cubes.
2. In a measuring cup, mix the pine needle syrup and cranberry juice.
3. Pour out the mixture evenly into the two glasses.
4. Top up with sparkling water and give it a gentle stir.
5. Decorate with fresh cranberries and a pine or spruce sprig.
6. Serve immediately and enjoy the festive cheer!

NUTRITIONAL INFORMATION

85 calories; 15g sugars; 0g protein; 20g carbohydrates; 0g fat; 0g fiber; 0mg cholesterol; 10mg sodium; 20mg potassium; Vitamin C: 20% of daily value.

APRIL'S APPLE ARDOR

2 servings | 10 minutes

EQUIPMENT

Shaker or Mixing Jug, Muddler, Strainer, Ice Cube Tray.

INGREDIENTS

- 2 medium-sized fresh apples, cored and sliced
- 1 oz elderflower syrup or elderflower liqueur
- 4 oz apple juice, preferably freshly pressed
- Soda water
- Ice cubes
- Apple slices and elderflower blossoms for garnish

DIRECTIONS

1. Muddle the apple slices at the bottom of the shaker to extract the juice.
2. Add elderflower syrup or liqueur and apple juice to the shaker.
3. Half-fill the shaker with ice crystals and vigorously shake until the drink is sufficiently chilled.
4. Pour the mixture into two glasses containing ice.
5. Top up with soda water to give it some fizz.
6. Garnish with a slice of apple and a few elderflower blossoms.

NUTRITIONAL INFORMATION

120 calories; 18g sugars; 0g protein; 30g carbohydrates; 0g fat; 0g fiber; 0mg cholesterol; 5mg sodium; 150mg potassium; Vitamin C: 20% of daily value.

MIDSUMMER MANGO MÉLANGE

🍴 2 servings 🕐 10 minutes

EQUIPMENT

Blender, Measuring cups, Strainer.

INGREDIENTS

- 1 cup ripe mango, peeled and cubed
- 1/2 cup passionfruit pulp
- 1 cup cold water
- 2 tbsp honey (or to taste)
- Ice cubes
- Fresh mango slices and passionfruit seeds for garnish

DIRECTIONS

#76

1. Place mango cubes, passionfruit pulp, water, and honey in the blender.
2. Blend until smooth and creamy.
3. If desired, strain the mix to remove any seeds or chunks.
4. Pour into glasses filled with ice.
5. Garnish with a mango slice and a sprinkle of passionfruit seeds.

NUTRITIONAL INFORMATION

210 calories; 30g sugars; 2g protein; 55g carbohydrates; 1g fat; 6g fiber; 0mg cholesterol; 10mg sodium; 500mg potassium; Vitamin C: 80% of daily value.

GOLDEN GOURD GALA

2 servings | 10 minutes

EQUIPMENT

Blender, Serving Glasses, Cinnamon stick for garnish.

INGREDIENTS

- ·1 cup roasted butternut squash puree
- ·2 cups almond milk (or preferred milk)
- ·1 tsp ground cinnamon
- ·1 tbsp honey (or to taste)
- ·A pinch of nutmeg
- ·A pinch of salt
- ·Ice cubes (optional)

DIRECTIONS

#77

1. In the blender, combine butternut squash puree, almond milk, cinnamon, honey, nutmeg, and salt.
2. Blend until smooth and creamy. If a cold beverage is preferred, add ice cubes and blend again until chilled.
3. Pour into serving glasses.
4. Garnish with a sprinkle of cinnamon on top and a cinnamon stick.

NUTRITIONAL INFORMATION

180 calories; 15g sugars; 2g protein; 25g carbohydrates; 4g fat; 3g fiber; 0mg cholesterol; 50mg sodium; 350mg potassium; Vitamin C: 25% of daily value.

VALENTINE'S VELVET VERVE

🍸 2 servings   🕐 15 minutes

EQUIPMENT

Blender, Saucepan, Glasses (preferably wine or cocktail glasses for an elegant touch).

INGREDIENTS

- 1 cup fresh strawberries, hulled and halved
- 2/3 cup milk or dairy-free alternative
- 1/2 cup semi-sweet chocolate chips
- 1 tsp vanilla extract
- Whipped cream for garnish
- Fresh strawberry slices and grated chocolate for decoration

DIRECTIONS

 #78

1. Constantly stir the chocolate morsels and milk together in a saucepan over low heat until smooth. Cool to room temperature after removing from fire.
2. In a blender, combine the strawberries, chocolate-milk mixture, and vanilla extract. Blend until smooth.
3. Pour out the mixture into glasses, leaving space at the top.
4. Decorate with whipped cream, fresh strawberry segments, and chocolate shavings.
5. Serve immediately and enjoy the sweet embrace of the flavors.

NUTRITIONAL INFORMATION

250 calories; 25g sugars; 4g protein; 30g carbohydrates; 10g fat; 3g fiber; 10mg cholesterol; 50mg sodium; 300mg potassium; Vitamin C: 60% of daily value.

HARVEST MOON HARMONY

🕯 2 servings   🕐 15 minutes

EQUIPMENT

Saucepan, Fine mesh strainer, Serving glasses.

INGREDIENTS

- ·2 large ripe pears, peeled and diced
- ·1.5 cups of water
- ·2 tsp whole cloves
- ·1 tbsp honey (adjust to taste)
- ·Ice cubes (optional)
- Pear slices and whole cloves for garnish

DIRECTIONS

#79

1. In a saucepan, combine diced pears, water, and whole cloves.
2. Bring the mixture to a boil, then reduce the heat to a simmer for approximately 5 minutes, or until the pears are tender.
3. Remove from heat and mash the pears to release their juices.
4. Strain the mixture into a pitcher, discarding the mashed pears and cloves.
5. Stir in honey to the strained liquid and adjust sweetness if necessary.
6. Let the drink cool, then refrigerate until chilled.
7. Garnish each glass with a clove and a slice of pear. To chill a beverage, serve it over ice.

NUTRITIONAL INFORMATION

100 calories; 20g sugars; 0.5g protein; 25g carbohydrates; 0.1g fat; 4g fiber; 0mg cholesterol; 10mg sodium; 150mg potassium; Vitamin C: 10% of daily value.

CITRUS SPARKLE SPLASH

🥄 1 servings   🕐 5 minutes

EQUIPMENT

Highball glass, Juicer, Stirrer

INGREDIENTS

- 1/2 Lemon
- 1/2 Lime
- 1-2 tsp Sugar (adjust to taste)
- 200ml Sparkling water
- 1 Fresh mint leaf

DIRECTIONS

#80

1. Squeeze the juice from the half lemon and half lime into the highball glass.
2. Add sugar to the glass and stir until dissolved.
3. Gently pour in the sparkling water, ensuring the effervescence is maintained.
4. Gently slap the mint leaf between your hands to release its aroma and place it atop the drink.
5. Stir gently to mix the flavors, and serve immediately.

NUTRITIONAL INFORMATION

40 calories; 10g sugars; 0g protein; 10g carbohydrates; 0g fat; 0g fiber; 0mg cholesterol; 1mg sodium; 30mg potassium; Vitamin C: 25% of daily value.

TROPICAL TANGO TWIRL

2 servings   10 minutes

EQUIPMENT

Blender, Citrus zester, Glasses

INGREDIENTS

- 2 cups pineapple juice
- 1 cup coconut cream
- Zest of 1 orange
- 2 cups crushed ice
- 2 cherries

DIRECTIONS

#81

1. Combine pineapple juice and coconut cream in the blender.
2. Add crushed ice to the mix.
3. Blend until you achieve a smooth consistency.
4. Pour into glasses and sprinkle with the zest of one orange.
5. Place a cherry on top as the finishing touch for each serving.

NUTRITIONAL INFORMATION

220 calories; 18g sugars; 2g protein; 28g carbohydrates; 10g fat; 1g fiber; 0mg cholesterol; 15mg sodium; 290mg potassium; Vitamin C: 70% of daily value.

RUBY RED RADIANCE

🍸 1 servings   🕐 6 minutes

EQUIPMENT

Glass, Juicer, Stirrer

INGREDIENTS

- 150ml Grapefruit juice
- 30ml Cranberry syrup
- 100ml Seltzer
- 1 Lime wedge
- 1 Rosemary sprig

DIRECTIONS

#82

1. Pour the grapefruit juice into the glass.
2. Add the cranberry syrup, stirring to mix.
3. Top up with seltzer and give a gentle stir.
4. Drop the lime wedge into the glass after squeezing it over the drink.
5. Garnish with a rosemary sprig.

NUTRITIONAL INFORMATION

85 calories; 16g sugars; 0g protein; 20g carbohydrates; 0g fat; 0g fiber; 0mg cholesterol; 15mg sodium; 200mg potassium; Vitamin C: 60% of daily value.

Enjoy

MELON MINT MARVEL

🧍 1 servings   🕐 6 minutes

EQUIPMENT

Blender, strainer, tall glass.

INGREDIENTS

- 4 oz Watermelon puree
- 6-8 Mint leaves
- 1 oz Lime juice
- 1 tbsp Honey
- 2 oz Soda water

DIRECTIONS

#83

1. In a blender, combine watermelon puree, mint leaves, lime juice, and honey. Blend until smooth.
2. Pour out the contents into a tall glass filled with ice.
3. Stir in the soda water gently.
4. Garnish with a sprig of mint and a wedge of lime.

NUTRITIONAL INFORMATION

90 calories; 18g sugars; 0g protein; 22g carbohydrates; 0g fat; 0.5g fiber; 0mg cholesterol; 5mg sodium; 100mg potassium; Vitamin C: 40% of daily value.

Enjoy

PEACHY KEEN COOLER

🍸 1 servings   🕐 6 minutes

EQUIPMENT

Glass, stirring rod

INGREDIENTS

- 3 oz Peach nectar
- 1 oz Lemon juice
- 1 tsp Honey
- 4 oz Iced tea
- 1 Sprig of thyme

DIRECTIONS

#84

1. In a glass, mix peach nectar, lemon juice, and honey until honey is dissolved.
2. Add iced tea and stir gently to combine.
3. Garnish with the sprig of thyme.

NUTRITIONAL INFORMATION

80 calories; 14g sugars; 0g protein; 20g carbohydrates; 0g fat; 0g fiber; 0mg cholesterol; 5mg sodium; 50mg potassium; Vitamin C: 45% of daily value.

Enjoy

CRISP CUCUMBER CALM

🤟 1 servings   🕐 6 minutes

EQUIPMENT

Glass, Juicer, Stirrer

INGREDIENTS

- 3-4 slices Cucumber
- 1 oz Lime juice
- 0.5 oz Simple syrup
- 8 oz Tonic water
- A pinch of Sea salt

DIRECTIONS   #85

1. At the bottom of the glass, muddle the cucumber slices.
2. Fill the glass halfway with lime juice and simple syrup.
3. Pour in the tonic water and give it a gentle stir.
4. Sprinkle the pinch of sea salt on top.

NUTRITIONAL INFORMATION

10 calories; 4g sugars; 0g protein; 1g carbohydrates; 0g fat; 0g fiber; 0mg cholesterol; 5mg sodium; 20mg potassium; Vitamin C: 5% of daily value.

Enjoy

BERRY BLISS BURST

🍸 1 servings   🕐 10 minutes

EQUIPMENT

Blender, Fine strainer, Glass

INGREDIENTS

- 1/2 cup Mixed berry puree
- Zest of 1/2 lemon
- 1 tablespoon Agave nectar
- 1 cup Club soda
- 1 Basil leaf

DIRECTIONS

#86

1. Blend the mixed berries to achieve a smooth puree.
2. Using a fine strainer, separate the puree from any seeds.
3. In the glass, mix berry puree, lemon zest, and agave nectar thoroughly.
4. Gently pour club soda into the mixture.
5. As a finishing touch, garnish with a basil leaf on top.

NUTRITIONAL INFORMATION

100 calories; 20g sugars; 1g protein; 25g carbohydrates; 0g fat; 3g fiber; 0mg cholesterol; 10mg sodium; 50mg potassium; Vitamin C: 50% of daily value.

Enjoy

GOLDEN GINGER GLIMMER

EQUIPMENT

Tall glass, Stirrer, Measuring cup

INGREDIENTS

- 200 ml Ginger ale
- 100 ml Apple juice
- 1 Lemon slice
- 1 tsp Honey
- A dash of Cinnamon

DIRECTIONS

#87

1. Pour the apple juice into the tall glass.
2. Add the honey and mix until it dissolves.
3. Slowly pour in the ginger ale to preserve its effervescence.
4. Gently float the lemon slice on top.
5. Finish by sprinkling a dash of cinnamon over the drink.

NUTRITIONAL INFORMATION

120 calories; 30g sugars; 1g protein; 31g carbohydrates; 0g fat; 3g fiber; 0mg cholesterol; 20mg sodium; 60mg potassium; Vitamin C:2% of daily value.

SUNNY STRAWBERRY SIP

🍓 1 servings   🕐 10 minutes

EQUIPMENT

Blender, Strainer, Tall Glass, Stirrer

INGREDIENTS

- 5-6 Fresh strawberries
- 100ml Orange juice
- 20ml Simple syrup
- 150ml Sparkling water
- 1 Twist of lemon

DIRECTIONS   #88

1. Blend the fresh strawberries to get a smooth puree.
2. In a tall glass, mix the strawberry puree with orange juice.
3. Add simple syrup to the mixture and stir well.
4. Fill the glass with sparkling water, leaving some space at the top.
5. Garnish with a twist of lemon.

NUTRITIONAL INFORMATION

127 calories; 27g sugars; 1g protein; 31g carbohydrates; 1g fat; 1g fiber; 0mg cholesterol; 10mg sodium; 45mg potassium; Vitamin C: 20% of daily value.

CONCLUSION

The world of mocktails, much like its spirited counterpart, is one rich with creativity, tradition, and innovation. As we draw this guide to a close, it's essential to reflect on the artistry and the passion that goes into crafting these non-alcoholic delights.

Mocktails are more than just a mixture of random juices and soda. They represent a conscious choice for many; a desire to relish in the beauty of a cocktail experience without the inebriation. This decision is not merely about abstention; it's about celebration — of flavors, occasions, and company.

The craftsmanship behind a good mocktail requires a keen understanding of flavors and the subtleties of how they interact. While alcohol often provides a base note around which other ingredients dance, in a mocktail, every component is both a lead performer and a supporting act. This demands a heightened sense of balance, where the sweetness of a fruit, the tang of citrus, or the fizz of soda must harmoniously coalesce.

Just like traditional cocktails, mocktails have stories to tell. Every stirred concoction, every muddled herb, brings with it a tale of origin, whether steeped in history or inspired by a contemporary event. When presented, a mocktail speaks of the bartender's journey, their influences, inspirations, and aspirations. It's a silent conversation between the creator and the consumer, a story told through sips and sighs of satisfaction.

As we conclude, remember that the art of mocktail crafting is ever-evolving. It's a canvas of infinite potential, bound only by the limits of imagination. Whether you're a professional bartender, a home enthusiast, or someone merely enjoying the drink, always be open to experimentation, learning, and most importantly, savoring every sip.

Now that you have the right knowledge, put it into practice. Delve into the world of mocktail creation with newfound confidence and enthusiasm. If this book was instrumental in elevating your mocktail crafting journey, we would be honored to hear from you. Please consider leaving a review to share your experiences and inspire others. Your feedback helps us continue our mission of sharing the art and passion of beverage crafting with the world. Thank you!

INDEX

Made in the USA
Las Vegas, NV
19 December 2024

14556734R00057